THE WORSHIP TEAM

The Worship Team

By Brent-Anthony Johnson

Noisy Tony Music & Publishing

Earth

Published 2012

By Brent-Anthony Johnson

Noisy Tony Music & Publishing

Copyright © 2012 - Brent-Anthony Johnson

Cover Design by Sasha M. Johnson

Photo by Sasha M. Johnson

THE WORSHIP TEAM
— By Brent-Anthony Johnson

Colossians 1:25-29

"I have become its servant by the commission God gave me to present to you the word of God in its fullness— the mystery that has been kept hidden for ages and generations, but is now disclosed to the Lord's people. To them God has chosen to make known among the Gentiles the glorious riches of this mystery, which is Christ in you, the hope of glory.

"He is the one we proclaim, admonishing and teaching everyone

with all wisdom, so that we may present everyone fully mature in Christ. To this end I strenuously contend with all the energy Christ so powerfully works in me."

New International Version (NIV) Bible [emphasis added]

Joel 2:17(B)

"Do not make your inheritance an object of scorn, a byword among the nations.

Why should they say among the peoples,' Where is their God?'"

New International Version (NIV) Bible [emphasis added]

"A painter paints pictures on canvas. But musicians paint their pictures on silence" – *Leopold Stokowski*

Author's Foreword

Writing this book was the most difficult undertaking of my life to date! I don't say that lightly, as I've worked in the area of teaching, writing and journalism in my field for a very long time! There were times during this painful process that I honestly wanted to give up and let go of the original idea. Let alone the fact that constant re-

writing of the entire content took the better part of 3 years. But…
that's enough about the matter and the attempt to collect far too
many thoughts into these very few pages of text. Thankfully, the
Holy Spirit was constantly by my side, and the worship I
experienced through this exercise was well worth the deep heart's
cry and constant **Romans 8:26** groaning.

Several of my closest friends also provided insight and prayers as
we journeyed together to accomplish this book. I truly leaned on
the strength of my friends while this writing process took hundreds
of hours to write… and to come to grips with. Thank you very
much for taking the time (and effort) to weed through this muddled
landscape. I truly pray you will find the treasure the Lord has so
playfully hidden in the following pages.

My wife has been very instrumental in smoothing out my
presentation of this material. In addition to being a loving wife and
mother, my beloved is a very loving and caring personality type
who truly believes that the point of this book should be stated. But
also, that I need *"a loooooot of work…"* in the area of how I speak
to this subject in print. Presentation is everything, I guess! The
experiences I hope to speak to are based entirely upon my 30+
years as a functioning, full-time musician – 25 years of that time,
to date, I have also been a married and sometimes struggling
provider for my wife and the family we have built together.

Tracy is not a musician. Though, she is an able sight-reader with a deep understanding of music that belies her absent professional participation. She enjoys music and all of the community aspects of musical worship, and she can do so even if the musical presentation is by all musical standards "poor". That isn't to say she completely ignores poor musical presentation. Nor is it to say, because she sleeps with a professional musician, that she deems herself worthy to participate on a worship team. She isn't one to overtly comment on the subject of music in a church, or any other, musical context. No. Never. Instead, Tracy is one of the most able children's pastors I have met in all of my life. These facets of ability and personality are merely a few of the many reasons I truly appreciate my closest friend and, often, lovingly harshest critic – both musically and in the area of my treatment of myself and of God's people as it pertains to the subject of music in the church.

As I have mentioned, the concept of this book has been with me for several years. As much as anything, when considering the task of writing this book, I didn't want to appear unnecessarily "judgmental" or "elitist" in any way. In the area of musical worship, and in some small Pauline attempt, I am leaning on I Corinthians 9:22: *"To the weak I became weak, to win the weak. I have become all things to all men so that by all possible means I might save some."* – in an attempt to deal correctly with church musical worship, and how this book could potentially be an important treatise on the subject.

Yes, I realize that the very subject and material in itself brings forth a lot of emotion and the asking of any comments pertaining to "why", "how", and the proverbial "who" is commonly bound in the obviously (though not necessary) negative responses and reactions of those I'm hoping to speak to about this monster we presently identify as musical worship in the church. Drat! I fully understand the latent consternation and trepidation surrounding this subject even as we embark upon this controversial conversation together. Because of the foreseeable danger I thank you, in advance, for your grace and consideration as I try to articulate the ideas the Lord has patiently laid upon my heart.

Maybe I'm called to write this. The overstated goal is not to offend or even to correct any fellowship's worship program or vision… only to speak to the matter of music, musicians (alleged and actual), and the use of music by the average church in the 21st Century. Thanks again!

Brent-Anthony Johnson

The Challenge

One of the goals of this book is to challenge the average "church player" in the average Evangelical church, in average America, to set their sights higher than they have bothered to consider heretofore; particularly in the areas of their personal participation and the preparedness that their participation requires from a Biblical standpoint.

The result of studying music by individual worship team participants can only enhance the overall worship experience from a musical standpoint, and it should in no way be considered a deficit of an individual who seeks to bring value to their worship team(s) and musical worship experience. As much as the individual's study of music there should also be a daily study of God's Word, and the pursuit of a personal relationship with Jesus Christ. These two seemingly separate facets should become the constant and consummate practice and pursuit of any person who seeks to participate in a musical worship environment.

The idea that musical knowledge somehow detracts from the movement of the Holy Spirit in worship is completely absurd, and the resulting profundity of accomplishment, calling, and God-gifted ability lies within the offering of each participant on any worship team. Musical knowledge does not lead to performance any more than Biblical knowledge leads to some strange and regular desire to speak to the congregation as its pastor or spiritual leader!

On the contrary, musical ability and Biblical understanding allows for complete understanding of one's calling, gifts, talents and duties. Along with understanding there comes an ease and natural ability in presentation that allows the emphasis on the player attempting to play to be altogether removed from the musical environment in the church.

Knowledge and understanding (or the lack thereof) clearly exposes the purpose of a participant's presence in the public gathering place. In other words, understanding our personal reasons for participating in any church leadership scenario allows for clarity of purpose - which lies deep in the heart of all persons who are driven to serve. I do not identify participating on the worship team as a "ministry". In truth, most church participation is a matter of "church leadership" far more than it is a ministry of any sort.

Imagine a pastor who has never studied the Bible, but who insists upon speaking to the congregation on a weekly basis. Why would such a thing ever be allowed, and who would follow such an ill prepared shepherd? Frankly, that sort of thing doesn't exist in a world where it's a valuable asset to understand, from both a technical and spiritual standpoint, what each of us are supposed to be doing in our service within Christ's body! Unfortunately, however, it is predominantly in the church atmosphere that this strange contrary thinking prevails in the area of music presentation; particularly in the realm of musical worship, which may be due to the average Church's large volunteer base and the consideration of people's time restraints and so on. Fair enough.

Having identified a probable cause of this upsetting "musical phenomena" in the church, which is due to an apparent lack of fruit being identified in the previous paragraphs. The church errs in considering an individual's busy work-a-day schedule more than the reason for that person's presence in what should be the working leadership structure of corporate worship within a fellowship.

The church is seemingly in a tailspin of attempting to produce good fruit that is fathered by poor musical/artistic seeds. We can never harvest healthy fruit through the current means by which we are planting and harvesting Biblically accomplished and musically able musicians, simply because the church isn't planting healthy seeds, in the area of music, to begin with.

Poor musicianship never gives birth to good musicianship. Ever. Poor Biblical and musical knowledge coupled with an utter lack of accountability and integrity will never give birth to a better situation, and it isn't the Lord's job to "fix" the problem. Our reasonable response to the Lord is to therefore bring proper worship in the proper way, particularly as it pertains to music and the presenters of that music.

God is love, and the love of God promotes a willingness to worship Him for who he is, and for his relentless desire to operate through our hands to meet the lost and to welcome one another in worship to himself.

If this is the case, my hope is to bring Christians back to the basics of why we're doing what we're doing in the area of musical worship, and who should (and potentially shouldn't) be working in the area of musical worship in the church.

Story

Christ reached out to me at the not-so-young age of 17. By that time, I had experienced too much of the fallen world by anyone's account. I had begun playing in adult "cover bands" at age 15 with much older musician types who found their home in the bar, drink, drug, and sex culture(s) associated with the "school of hard knocks". So, by 17, I had an unadvisable working knowledge of that world. I don't suggest this particular approach to dealing with earth, by the way. Honestly, I learned a lot… But, I don't suggest that route! I saw addiction, violence, and death. Real and actual death and definitely more than I should have experienced at that, or any, age.

In addition to witnessing the dismal lives of most of my fellow bandmates, I had been born to teenage parents and I was convinced that I was destined to father a child, lose my dream of being a music professional and all that it entails, and ultimately begin an inescapable downward spiral of awful relationships, horrible living conditions, and cheap, lousy food – just like the guys I was hanging out with.

I also thought of myself as a mistake by birth, before my personal Christ experience, and that's not a great place to start from. But, that sounds a lot like the fallen world we all come from, doesn't it?

Christ alone has since repaired my relationship with my wonderful parents, and only He has healed the wounds of living my first nearly 2 decades of life as a self-viewed (often proclaimed and nearly self-appointed) accident. Maybe that's another book! Maybe I don't care enough to write it… unless I'm told to do so. Come quickly, Lord Jesus!

Meeting the Lord was a wonderful experience, and the first few months were spent wrapped in His nearly crushing presence as I read His Word and prayed for hours each day. I ran as far and as fast I could from the polluted, fallen world I had come from! My hunger for all things musical was quelled for a period as I walked and talked with my Savior. Though I continued to study and practice music, I spent much more time learning of God's love for me through His Word! I am His forever! Me? Really? I belong to someone who understands this person who might have been made for some purpose? <u>THE</u> Someone loves me? Not only that, but He wanted me! Cool! I'm all in!

Don't misunderstand me... my parents have always loved and wanted me. But I have to admit, as far as my flesh and blood parents are concerned, I have never been truly understood. I was "different" in so many ways from them on a deep level. Not special. Simply, I was not a part of anyone... and very much apart from everyone in an overt way. Remnants of that remain as my struggle to this day, as it does in so many of the truly called and actual musicians and artists I've met and befriended over the years. For his part, the Lord continues to reign in my heart, mind, and life. I was a little sad that he didn't completely take away the sarcasm and cynicism. He seems to use it, somehow! In Christ, I felt loved and made for an actual and specific purpose. That was the first time I heard the Holy Spirit say, "you're a musician, and I meant that - for now and for eternity." The new season of my life began in earnest!

And then...

Then, I began to meet the church and church people. More so, I began to meet those who specifically and proudly wore the title of "church player", which was entirely different from myself - a young, growing and very serious music student. They were also very different from the bar musicians I knew so well, or those truly professional (and actual) musicians I was beginning to work with more regularity outside the church walls.

These "church players" were people who really felt it was their God-given right to know nothing about music and to flaunt the fact through a veil of false humility and pugnacious ignorance toward their craft! It was all 'grace' and 'freedom', and no accountability. These folks weren't in any way 'players' and they had no deep sense of musical purpose, like those I knew who fed their families through music! I had never met people like these before, and I was confused and terrified. I wanted nothing to do with this oddball clique!

Once again, it is the Lord who has so wonderfully mended my strained relationship with these often very wantonly ignorant church players. Now, I can look back on those early days and see the sense of humor the Lord has and the strong sense of understanding, and even grace, he has built into me through adversity. I have since heard the Lord laugh with me about those earliest experiences with church players.

Like many virile, young, talented boys I met Jesus through a girl. These pages cannot contain the complete weirdness of that particular relationship. But, suffice to say, the girl was trying really hard to see to it that I immersed myself in the Christian culture in order to save my soul from hell… through the particularly silly and pointless exercise of "getting rid of all secular music" in exchange for the Christian albums of the day. Does anyone remember that shockwave that ran through the Body a few decades ago? YIKES!

At first, I worked really hard to enjoy and appreciate the music I was hearing. I tried. Hard. But, there was so much real musicality and musical integrity lacking in those records that I couldn't do it! I didn't get it, and I didn't want it. I had to have real music and I deeply craved something of musical substance for a grand total of 14 months as I searched for something substantial in that less-than-interesting world of popular Christian music. I wont mention any names here. But, suffice to say that this was the early 1980s, and the scant product that existed sounded an awful lot like really bad versions of tunes I knew well! That was the era of "they're a Christian (version) of…!" Remember that? No thank you, I'd rather listen to…!

I began to ask myself why was I bothering to listen to these apparently inept impersonators of actual music instead of just listening to music! Was it 'holy' because they kept saying the Lord's Name - the Name above all names? I couldn't make that idea work in my head. I tried. Hard. I prayed. Hard. I fasted. I sought the Lord for the answer to my question, "Obviously, this is about You – at least, lyrically. But… why is this 'music' so half-hearted at best? Why is much of it still so much so?"

When I had finally taken more than I could bear, I began asking my new Christian friends if they knew who some of these artists and bands were imitating. I also began rebuilding my 'secular music collection' and I would often play the original song that the Christian tune my friends were so enamored with was attempting to emulate. I received a lot of blank stares and, at one point, my loving new family of believers surrounded me as they earnestly prayed for my obviously damned soul. I cringe as I remember one of them praying, "release him (me) music! You can't have him! He (me) belongs to the Lord!"

As a result of my queries and obvious "fun-making" of the Christian subculture and especially Christian music, the girl went away and my friends melted into the landscape. So, I continued to seek the Lord, and I continued to play and study music.

I went on in my young life to begin an in depth study of music and of the Bible, both formally and privately. Throughout my younger life, particularly as I participated in Christian music projects and in church worship teams, the regular inquisition of my mode of dress, jewelry choices, hairstyles, and even the choice of how I wore my musical instrument would be in question and under regular scrutiny by this subculture. Humorously, though tragically, I was once asked to resign from playing at a church because of how I wore my instrument, and because I groove. Really.

Though I could go on-and-on about this… the thing I learned most about the church is that Christian music isn't about music at all! More than that, it certainly isn't about creative and/or true musical ability or expression. Hence, the book! It's where I belong, I guess… writing this type of thing. I am a Christian and I also work in the secular music community. It doesn't bother me to be, more often than not, the only Christian In the environment I work in. My witness lies in my ability to play well, and in my treatment of fellow human beings from all walks of life. Jesus loves them too, and it is due to my ongoing practice and study of music that witnesses to the musicians and audiences I work with – Christian, or not. Plainly put: I worship my Lord and Savior, regardless of the musical environment. Shouldn't all Christian musicians do that? More to the matter: is music played in the church somehow different than all other music? With that, should the expectations and abilities of musicians who play in a church environment be any different (any less) than musicians who play in any other environment?

Chapter 1

What is musical worship from a Biblical perspective?

Ephesians 5:15-20

"Be very careful, then, how you live—not as unwise but as wise, making the most of every opportunity, because the days are evil. Therefore do not be foolish, but understand what the Lord's will is. Do not get drunk on wine, which leads to debauchery. Instead, be filled with the Spirit, speaking to one another with psalms, hymns, and songs from the Spirit. Sing and make music from your heart to the Lord, always giving thanks to God the Father for everything, in the name of our Lord Jesus Christ."

New International Version (NIV) Bible [emphasis added]

Psalm 100:2

"Worship the LORD with gladness; come before him *with joyful songs."*

New International Version (NIV) Bible [emphasis added]

Psalm 107:21-22

"Let them give thanks to the Lord for his unfailing love and his wonderful deeds for men. Let them sacrifice thank offerings and *tell of his works with songs of joy."*

New International Version (NIV) Bible [emphasis added]

James 5:13 "Is anyone happy? Let him *sing songs of praise."*

New International Version (NIV) Bible [emphasis added]

Colossians 3:16 "Let the word of Christ dwell in you richly as you teach and admonish one another with all wisdom, and *as you sing psalms, hymns and spiritual songs with gratitude in your hearts to God.*"

New International Version (NIV) Bible [emphasis added]

Psalm 33:3 *"Sing to him a new song; play skillfully, and shout for joy."*

New International Version (NIV) Bible [emphasis added]

In 44 of the 66 books of the Bible, music is mentioned and spoken to at length by God, beginning with the Psalm of Creation in Genesis. As you are probably aware, the book of Psalms is the most expansive display of musical worship in the entire Bible. However, singing and the act of musical worship occur throughout the entire Bible as a whole. Countless examples of singing, playing music, and even the description of musical ability are given in many examples in God's Word. David was brought to Saul due to his musical ability, for example. Luke's Gospel includes Mary's singing response to her calling to birth the Christ through the *Magnificat* (1:46–55), the *Benedictus* (1:68–79), Gloria in *Excelsis Deo* (2:14), and *Nunc Dimittis* (2:29–32).

It is more than a little obvious that God loves music and He's graciously given the gift of music to humankind for our benefit and joy! When we play and sing we experience one of the Lord's great pleasures! Praise the Lord!

We are called (far more than encouraged) to be a singing, dancing, worshiping people in our thanks to and praise of the Lord God Almighty, and the how, what, and why we should sing are spoken to at length throughout the Word of God. It is also strongly implied that many prophecies were sung to the nations of Israel and Judah, and a number of Israel's contests, like Jericho, were won through musical worship. Even if the church has ignored the fact, music is an incredibly powerful tool! That tool can draw people to the Gospel of Christ. Or, if used improperly, music can repel people from our God! This is no laughing, or faint, matter. Particularly since the responsibility of the use of this tool is often largely overlooked by the average church.

The focus of this book is driven by the aforementioned Psalm 33:3 "Sing to him a new song; play skillfully, and shout for joy."

This book speaks more to the *"play skillfully"* aspect of the scripture, and I'm hoping to unpack several ideas pertaining to why the church has become what it has become in the area of music (specifically), and how to begin walking the path toward regaining an area that has been lost in our witness to a dying world. The solution to bettering our musical witness lies within us – far beyond the thought that it is our Lord's duty to miraculously change the hearing of the multitude of potential listeners we have been called to reach.

The Attitude of Our Musical Offering

Most of us in the church know the story of Cain and Abel. Lets take a moment to speculate the differences in the offering these two men made to God Almighty, and why God refused Cain's offering. Yes, I understand that blood had something to do with the matter. I'm speaking to the potentially overlooked aspects of this very swift and potentially mysterious read in Genesis.

As a concept, I propose that Abel not only presented "the best" of his livestock while Cain simply brought an offering of whatever was available. But, additionally, there may be a lingering thought that Cain never properly prepared himself or his offering – as any true preparation entails a great deal of work that he simply wasn't up to doing for God, or for anyone else, as it appears. Perhaps, Cain was overly busy with the appearance of trying to raise produce, while not truly working to do so. Is it a stretch to say he was, maybe, too busy to be bothered with bringing his absolute best through hard work and sacrifice to Almighty God? Perhaps God's rejection was far more about Cain's attitude than the offering itself. That isn't a stretch to consider, is it? Or, maybe this situation and why it lives in the holy Word of God, is more about our attitude than any offering we may bring to the Lord.

So, possibly, Cain didn't bring his best to God for a number of potentially valid (though fallen) human reasons. For instance, perhaps Cain wanted to retain the best of his produce for his own table. Or, Cain wasn't able to understand how important it is to prepare for the sacrifice God requires far in advance of the actual event? Could this story contain an aspect of his poor attitude? Or, maybe Cain simply didn't enjoy farming? Certainly many pastors, theologians and speakers have spoken to this subject, and I don't pretend to be any of these learned persons. But, there is something insidious about Cain's headspace, and that speaks beyond the idea of simply making an offering. That is the matter I hope to speculate on in these pages.

We can all agree that sacrifice is something more than simply bringing some sort of 'gift' and laying it before God, and that the idea of preparation is an interesting thing to consider in this conjectured scenario. That said, one thing is certain: Both Can and Abel were human. Both men were consumed by the needs of life such as providing shelter and protection, and making sure there was enough food to eat in order to sustain their own survival even if their personal survival isn't the apparent point of this story.

In our adult lives, our jobs (not our calling, by-and-large) provide shelter, food, and even protection for ourselves and for our families. So then, where does calling fit into our lives and how do we manage our time so that our calling is first identified and then properly nurtured? I want to plant the seed in your mind that it is largely possible that your calling isn't for your personal use as much as it is for the Lord's desire to attract humankind to himself. So, very much as it is with a calling to participate in the infant and toddler ministry, the calling to participate on the worship team has little (if anything) to do with your personal love of playing music; *playing* musician, or seeking a position within your fellowship, as much as it has to do with the preparation he has purposely engineered to achieve his goals for his purpose.

More likely than not, the Lord has a plan to use you in the environment he's placed you in! You need to be acutely aware of this fact, and potentially begin making yourself ready for him doing so. If the goal of worship team participation is service, then we should strive to bring that "special" thing that is beyond our schedules, and our personal timeline, to our fellowship. This can only be achieved by a lifestyle that is in focused participation with the Lord's calling and his ongoing work in us for the local body we are called to lead.

Several scriptures give us a hint about the "dirty diapers" (infant ministry anyone?) each of us is called to deal with within the context of our personal calling. It's called *preparation* and every calling has a pile of potentially unpleasant duties inherent alongside the joy of answering the call. Naturally, I will bring this back around to the potentially dirty diaper of your personal, daily, private music practice and whether or not you're meeting the Lord at the place he's calling you to.

Imagine how many children some of us would parent if there were no physical labor, and no need to provide shelter, food, or protection for those children we could then call "our own"? In addition to the Lord's calling there is responsibility and equally stern warnings if the call is taken lightly – even after accepting the Lord's mandate into our hearts and then setting out on the path to achieve those things the Lord has said, "do". I have to comment here how humorous and interesting it is that a particular parable refers to personal gifts as "talents". Take a moment to consider your use of the talent the Lord has given you, and then read the scathing response of misusing talents in Matthew 25:14-30 and Luke 19:12-28. What happens when we don't properly employ and invest our talents? Standing on the church platform and being musically obnoxious is not "investment" by any means!

Unfortunately, after the initial run toward the task(s) given to us by the Holy Spirit, many simply run out of steam, or become complacent in lost direction and purpose. Many of us settle into a "well, that's life" response of failing to meet the goals we felt so important at one time, or another. We must remain mindful of those aspects of our calling that need constant maintenance in order for us to be relevant witnesses in our quickly changing world. Because, like it or not, our witness is out there in that constantly changing environment! Furthermore, if the Lord supplies for all our needs, is it acceptable to rely on the Lord's understanding of our busy lives… even if we are called to focus on his tasks for us above working our jobs? No one's job is his or her life, by-and-large. Yet, the calling and the related sacrifice we're called to make, for the Lord's service, is too often paled by those things we have convinced ourselves is the point of living. Having and gaining, is not the point. So, what would happen if we realized that the Lord alone has given us all we have, and our focus in this regard is unnecessary? That isn't to say, "don't work". The question is, "what are you focusing on in your life?

Removing the issue of what we "own" leaves us with the purpose of his calling in our lives. If you are called to be a musician for his sake, the focus needs to be there instead of how great we look on the platform at church, and what that implies to the uninitiated and ignorant. The focus may need to be redirected to substance and content. Not presence. At no point does one's presence negate duty, and duty begins with acceptance and a correct attitude after accepting the Lord's call to task.

If a worship team participant neglects to identify and include the "dirty diapers" of study, practice, and the gaining of musical knowledge through intent and purpose… they are probably not called to serve as musicians for Christ. Or, maybe they've failed to understand what they're supposed to be doing while serving in the capacity of "worship musician" in the church. Matthew 25:14-30 and Luke 19:12-28 are a clear reminder of how we are to deal with our gifts!

More About Cain and Abel

The thought of Abel and his offering reminds me of what it means to prepare oneself for a personal offering to the Lord. It rings true that Abel had a God-given knowledge of livestock, just as Cain had a strong working knowledge of crops and fieldwork. So Abel's preparation possibly began with not simply the end result of the offering, but with the choosing of the animals and feed that would produce the best offspring that would finally then produce the best offering. Maybe Abel anticipated the bringing of an offering to God by planning the offering's end-result… and, maybe, he did so years in advance of the actual act of worship though purposed sacrifice! Maybe, it all began with an acknowledged gift from God Almighty, like a great pair of animals that Abel understood would potentially bring forth strong and virtually spotlessly and healthy offspring!

We read about an interesting correlation to this matter of God's blessing a faithful man through the use of livestock in the life of Jacob (Genesis 30:32-35) and how the Lord blessed Jacob over Laban through prompting Jacob to select something of less aesthetic value that God could use to glorify Himself. In reading this account of Jacob, it is very easy to overlook the difficult and purposeful work Jacob must have lent to the task. In the same way, we must realize that buying a musical instrument does not produce musical skill anymore than owning volumes of literarily works produces functional knowledge of the library's content.

Very often, we are called upon to nurture something seemingly insignificant (an initial gift or small talent) that the Lord then blesses into the use of His holy purposes. If we're given a self-assessed or self-proclaimed "little talent", the idea may be to work hard to grow it beyond our assumptions and expectations as a witness to God's faithfulness. That often requires work that begins with the understanding of nurturing the gift beyond "just as it is", even if each of us are received by the Lord "just as I am".

Each of us is individually called upon to some manner of sacrificial task beyond "showing up for Jesus". I suggest that the answer to who we are in Christ, and the job we were given to accomplish, lies in that thing we long to give to the Lord. I also suggest that whatever it happens to be, it should require a great deal of work to bring that gift into the fruition the Lord longs to see in each of us. There is no "showing up for Jesus" without taking on the responsibility of seeing the Lord's goals into fruition – first in ourselves, and then as a witness of his love in the world we live in.

As I speculate through the matter and content of this story, and what it might mean… Maybe Abel's offering was planned and intentionally worked toward after accepting God's initial gift and/or call. From that point, it would take a longer period of time to achieve Abel's goal to produce an offering than previously considered. Again, these are only thoughts. But there is something to be said for purposely and intentionally bringing the Lord our best, and that our best may not be something that generally happens 'at the moment', contrary to popular belief.

Bringing the Lord our absolute best isn't about what's in our pockets on any given day, with the exception of our brokenness and hardened hearts – even if our God can use all things to bring glory to Himself!

The church seem to throw a lot of its musical offering at God from whatever intent happens to be in its shallow pockets from Sunday-to-Sunday, instead of having a long-term goal that can only be achieved through each individual's responsibility to move a musical vision into fruition. Being on the worship team isn't about position or title, as much as it is about specific, ongoing preparation and intentionality. Without any doubt, we are to come humbly before the Lord in worship. However, if we are to use the tool of music properly, we cannot forsake the proper understanding of the tool in our hands and how to use it. <u>Ignorance does not equal humility</u>!

As a resulting practice of long-term position seeking and entitlement within the church, the musical offering (as far as it goes) seems to be weak, unprepared, and far more about the person making the offering than to whom the offering is for. This fact stems from an absolutely upside down thought process.

Once again, let's go back to Cain and his younger brother Abel…

It obviously takes a great deal of hard work to guard the soil against weeds and harmful insects and to properly fertilize the seed that would bring forth the best produce. These are many things that must be done in advance, if the proper yield is to come forth. It also rings true that possibly Cain didn't fully understand that he was offering something of great value to God. That is: Time, effort and response to the Lord's worthiness.

Time and worship are both very important ingredients in the recipe of offering. Weeding is also very important in this regard, and ignoring it may produce a weak offering. No one truly knows if Cain weeded his garden, or not. But, there's something about his attitude that cannot be denied. Though the Lord's burden is easy and His yoke is light, the time spent with the Lord in preparation and for His purposes is never an act of happenstance or serendipitous accident. Weeding is important. It's one of those "dirty diaper" situations that cannot be ignored and must be dealt with. Often, the time spent in deep preparation and study is the greatest gift we receive from the Lord – as we participate with him for an end he has in mind. Even if it feels like weeding our gardens, instead of spending quality time with our Father in heaven! In other words, the commission of a worshiping musician isn't about the reward of being identified as a member of the worship team! It is about weeding in the area of our daily practice and understanding of our assignment. To many of my Christian students I refer to daily musical practice as "sword sharpening", and I remind them that it's entirely up to them whether or not their sword will be sharp on the day it may be called for! Cute, isn't it? As long as it makes sense, I'll use any silly analogy or metaphor!

From what I understand (very little at best) farming and ranching are both very difficult work – especially after the Genesis curse on the earth and the fall of humankind! Yet, Abel, who also knew the curse and fully understood the definition of toil and the raising of livestock, contended to produce something of great sacrificial value to present as his offering – possibly after years of preparation. While Cain may only have thought to bring "what he had at the moment", and perhaps without making the proper earlier preparations that results in great crops! Again, these are only thoughts based upon the arrogant response we read from Cain in Genesis.

You know where I'm going here… Instead of witnessing groups of actual practicing musicians in the church, who work hard on their craft in order to bring something of great value to our calling, there is instead a resulting scenario that smacks of Cain's arrogance in the area of the weekly displayed lackluster musical preparation and presentation. More so, there is a deeply jealous attitude in the average church player that longs to "kill Abel", in the embodiment of true musicianship and actual musical calling, toward those bringing something of investment and hard work to offer to the Lord! I can't tell you how many times I have witnessed the repeated slaying of Abel's heart by average church players who have never bothered to become true musicians, let alone having the mind set to bring a proper offering or a sacrifice of praise to the Lord through hard work and preparation. I honestly can't tell you how many times I've witnessed this – as it is too numerous to recount!

We've all heard the words; "I was too busy (with work, with my children, with my life…) to learn the songs (let alone worship through them) this week", from the mouths of worship team members – typically those members who need the most practice! But, out of an incorrect sense of 'love', the church simply and continuously allows this lack of preparation to the extent of it being the rule above the exception.

The resulting fruit of poor musicianship, poorer preparation and misguided understanding of the purpose of participation is another small reason why we live in a "post-Christian" or "post-modern" age where the chasm between the world and Christ's people grows wider and wider with each passing year. Yes, Jesus Christ is the perfect sacrifice, and He alone made a way for all men to approach God Almighty. However, that fact doesn't let us "off the hook" in the matter of our personal witness before the world.

The church is throwing an awful lot of "bless this mess" at the world and, quite frankly, the world simply doesn't get it, or want it. If we are the body of Christ, we need to seriously re-think how we're representing Christ through our actions within the church and in the world! Particularly those actions that involve seeking entitlement, lame excuses, and self-congratulatory weirdness the church has become all too well known for by the world at large.

After playing a performance or session with a non-Christian I have experienced the response, "but… you play so well!" when I inform the artist of my faith in Christ! Believe it, or not, that indictment is very common in my life experience! That response speaks volumes to what the world thinks of the music coming out of the doors of the average church, doesn't it? It also speaks to why those musicians aren't showing up at the local church on any given Sunday morning.

Other than obscuring our Lord and Savior through lousy music, musical ignorance and self-centeredness, what is the average church bringing to this sea of dying and damned people in this area of music - beyond those Christian musicians who, like myself, work in the secular music environment? Why do a large percentage of the non-Christian musicians in towns across this country think so poorly of "church players"? For many of those people I've met outside the church, each has a story that sounds a lot like, "yeah... my sister (brother, grandmother, friend) is a Christian and she invited me to church because they think the music is 'really good'. It isn't! I couldn't go there."

If music is a tool that churches insist upon using, how are we effectively accomplishing the objective? What bait are we fishing with, and is it effective? Is what we're doing something that works well? Or, are we just wasting time?

A professional fisherman will tell you when you're fishing with the wrong bait, right? Only a truly cruel expert would allow you to spend your day in frustration and then go home empty-handed. So, in the form of this book... to whom much is given, much is required. We should dig in and honestly re-think our motives and approach!

Most of the outside world looks upon the musical worship portion of the church service with a general sense of, "what are they doing?" that isn't so much about the mentioning of the name of Jesus, as it is about the presentation of the music itself. Which is far too often pretty stinky at best. So the question begs to be asked, "what (or who) is the church hoping to catch with the bait being used?" Or, "what good work is the average church worship team doing to introduce strangers (let alone potential musical participants) to Jesus?"

I heartily insist that the church is supposed to be the best at musical presentation on earth - even if the pastor doesn't like it and he feels "in competition" with any great presentation… other than those that feature his/her face!

In this area, the church seems to be particularly encumbered by the ignorant pursuit of entitlement, infighting, lethargy and apathy. So much so, that a great portion of the original mission is left undone.

As a part of the many clinics I've been blessed to present on the subject of music, over many years, I often pose the question, "Was Jesus an able and gifted carpenter, and do you think Jesus approached carpentry in any way like the average church player approaches their musical calling?"

Surely, you understand that there is nothing written in the Bible about Jesus' carpentry, and there have been a few somewhat recent considerations that Jesus wasn't Joseph's eldest and the he wasn't responsible to inherit the family business. But, we know that Joseph was a carpenter, and that Jewish culture of that time-period (generally speaking) raised sons to follow the family trade. Right? Okay. Jesus is referred to as "the carpenter's son" and the prevailing thought is that Jesus was himself a carpenter. Was Jesus a good carpenter?

Why do I feel very confident that Jesus was a great woodworker – even if carpentry wasn't the purpose of his life anymore than music is the complete point of the church's presentation of God's Word to humankind? Why then should music be poorly presented instead of not presented at all as part of the average Sunday morning service? Why is it 'okay' that in most churches the desire to participate as a member of a worship team has become so much more about position than the purpose of leading from actual calling?

Worship pastors and/or worship leaders are supposed to do the job of teaching and leading in this particular area, aren't they? Does James 3:1 apply to the worship leader/worship pastor in its regard to leadership? Is anyone raising-up anyone to do anything in our churches in the area of music? Are there any teaching worship leaders in the church, and are they suggesting that taking music lessons from qualified teachers is a wonderful idea?

In nearly three decades, I have met less than a handful of worship leaders who encourage the best from the volunteers on their teams. I can honestly count only three such worship leaders I've met, and my memory is very sharp! This shouldn't be the case. But, unfortunately, it is so! And we wonder why the Lord isn't bringing great musicians to our humble fellowship, or why strangers aren't beating down the doors to hear "our really good worship team".

This matter looks a lot like an integrity problem that is based in an accountability problem in the hearts of all fallen humankind… who also just happen to be Christians. Yes, we're really that broken, even inside the church walls! Yet, those outside the church are very able to identify the fact that certain things are going on within the church that they don't want to have anything to do with – bad music being one of those things! All the while, on Sunday-after-Sunday, the worship team bumbles along from one badly presented song to another as some type of oddball team building exercise for their fellowship, their worship team(s) and more so for themselves. The world isn't playing the game of "because we're

Christians, everything we do is wonderful", and the proof is the fact that we're not winning in this battle for the hearts and souls of all people. The tool of well-presented music is as important as preaching, if we're going to win the hearts of the un-churched.

The point of using music to edify the body is completely moot, if the doors are open to anyone who may wander by! The world has closed the door on bad church music, leaving the church to enjoy it alone. Bad bait equals no fish. At best, poorly presented music merely attracts other untrained instrument owners who (at best) have an attitude of "heck, I can do that."

As I've mentioned, it isn't the Lord's job to bless the mess of the average church's weekly musical presentation. And, more often than not… He doesn't! True, sometimes He shows up – because He can! But, does the occasional visit from the Holy Spirit account for the many times the musical presentation is not tolerated by potential visitors as much as it is merely survived by the congregation? What about those unfortunate guests who unwittingly find themselves in this apparently private club meeting of jockeying position seekers who aren't thinking about musical presentation or calling at all… and who are on the team simply to be seen as important enough to be there? Does this issue of misused talent diminish our effectiveness once we go back into the world that surrounds the church walls?

Poor musical presentation dwindles into nothing more than a fellowship's weekly corporate entertainment, and the problem of why fewer and fewer actual musicians stay after initially coming through the doors is rampant as much as it is unanswered, or even cared about, by the people occupying positions. This fact continues to be ignored by pastors, worship leaders and the church player alike.

Something has to change here. Ooh, I know… let's begin offering great musical presentation! Would better presentations of all kinds make us more effective in our world? I believe so. If people come through the doors because the music and arts presentations are incredible SO BE IT! What's wrong with this idea – other than the hard work it takes to accomplish the task?

In order to insure better musical presentation from growing musicians who are seeking the Lord through his Word, worship leaders will need to become more invested in the lives of their players and their musical progress, and to speak openly to this never-ending debate of "great music by great players who love the Lord", over the allegedly "great hearted", who are generally spiritually clueless in addition to being musically worthless. Neat. Let's do more of that… it's easier than accomplishing the mission. Right?! Wrong. Dead wrong.

We are all very busy people in this world, and we will most likely always have a reason to cast a blind eye and excuses to the run amok situation of poor music in the average church. True, the end-result is that most churches continue to fail in the area of musical presentation in worship because very few volunteer church players understand their job as it pertains to this idea of knowledge, responsibility, calling and the sacrifice of that learned skill.

Can we truly sacrifice a talent we've never nurtured and purposely crafted into something of usefulness and worth to our witness? Not of worth to God, in the truest sense, but of value to our fellowship and those we're trying to reach with the goodness of Christ's love? Can we truly afford to be the filthy weirdoes who insist the world wipe its feet and wash its hands before entering our 'sacred' environment? Or, have we finally learned that they're not coming? Maybe they're not coming because there is nothing compelling about what we're doing. Maybe, it's the yucky musical presentation that partially convinces the world to just stay home – and listen to really good music there instead.

Have we asked ourselves why they aren't coming, understood why this is the case, repented, and sought the Lord's plan for bringing them in to hear His Word? Most worship teams have no qualms about running to some public stage to perform as an "outreach". But, how many teams have prepared the offering they're hoping to use to win these souls? How many individuals on those teams understand that appearing at some public place works only if there has been individual preparedness beyond simply praying that the Lord shows up? Most Christian music events I've attended haven't even offered passable tuning skills! This is an utterly shameful, and completely true fact for ninety percent of every provincial Christian music event I've bothered to attend. Without the exception of an occasional mighty move of God, the average Christian in the average church and town is only fooling themselves if they believe the world will beat down their door to meet our Jesus because, "I heard the music!"

The average provincial and even regional Christian outdoor music event can be compared to being invited to a banquet and after arriving finding that none of the food has actually been prepared! Oh, it's there... sort of. But, it isn't "ready" by any means! The tables are set, but there's no smell of cooking food. Instead, the groceries are just piled on the tables. No one likes to stand around a table of raw, smelly, germ-ridden uncooked meat, do they? I mean, even if the invitations for the event look nice, and everyone is friendly enough... No. Sooner, or later, a banquet comes down to the food. You know... THE FOOD! If the food is inedible it doesn't matter how well the promised "secret special wonderful dessert" has been advertised! Plainly, not many strangers are going to suffer through something unpleasant in hopes of receiving something better afterward. True?

Do you think the church is operating on some sort of long lost trust factor that was ignored and then diminished in effectiveness long, long ago? Do you think there have been too many bad Christian music events to entice the world back for another tenuous visit to the Christian stage? I wonder.

The church cannot continue to blame the lost for not staying around for the Word, if they're going to have to suffer through hours of really bad music in order to finally hear Christ's message – a message they don't know they need! It isn't Jesus' fault they don't come, any more than it's his desire to let them perish where they are. We Christians have a lot more responsibility than we're assuming in our witness.

Chapter 3

Our job as worship team participants is to present musical worship that allows the congregation to worship unhindered. It isn't about "show" – lights, stage presentation, or visual effects. Yes, churches use these devices regularly without actually ever dealing with building teams of able musicians who function in a called capacity! Musical worship is about the clear presentation of music by musician-worshipers who are growing in the understanding of their calling and purpose – as much as it is about the congregation's worship. If that is the case (and it is) then the important issues point directly to the players who are themselves participating on the worship team. Music is music. It's either well presented, or poorly presented. That is all. Poorly played music diminishes our witness. Whereas well-played music provides the platform for a positive introduction to the Lord we serve, and it speaks clearly to what we believe and to whom we believe we are in Christ. We cannot offer half-hearted presentation and expect anyone to take it seriously. True? So, like Cain, it's the headspace of the average church player that ignores what their actions actually mean to those observing them. The fact is we've not been given the privilege of witnessing to the world without the responsibility of doing it well and with prepared ability offered in appropriate humility.

Koinonia

As worship team members, we should focus first upon encouraging those weaker members of our team(s) toward greater musical and Biblical accountability beyond merely being on the team. What could the average team in an average church do with a deeper understanding of both the Lord's Word and music? If the team understands its task, it can then present its service to the congregation. Corporate worship isn't about the worship team's visual function any more than it is about learning the song "on the platform" on a given Sunday morning! The worship team's job is to remove themselves sacrificially so that the congregation can worship unhindered!

That may require team members who have worshiped to the set of music and practiced their instrument through the set in their homes prior to presenting them on the platform of their church. That may require those persons to get with their instrument and begin crafting the song into a personal song of worship as part of their weekly practice regimen. That is not to say that ignoring the other aspects of musical practice for the sake of the weekly church set is an acceptable musical approach. Not at all! As I've stated previously, a lack of musical knowledge and ability doesn't equal humility or worshipfulness on anyone's part. The only way to accomplish clear musical presentation is for each participating individual to understand their personal role in music to the extent of actually leading through their musical ability.

I have never witnessed a church player decline from playing on their worship team due to their lack preparedness. Never. There are too many unprepared players running to the platform, and the result is damaging to both the congregation and to the rest of the team. All the while the idea of declining in such a situation is sheathed in the false humility of, "but I loooove to worship!"

No. That simply means, "I love to be seen as a worshiper, and I love to be thought of as a musician"… whether or not they've actually prepared for the task of leading the congregation into worship before the Lord Almighty.

"You mean… we're supposed to be good musicians?!?"
"You mean we're supposed to be a 'team' that prays for one another and holds one another accountable for the sake of leading the congregation of our church?"

That's right. The church is supposed to be the one place in our lives where everything presented is done well. Through accomplishing this, we will begin to hear the lost question, "why does this work?" instead of the all too familiar words from the bewildered observers in the world, "why doesn't this work?" or, "what are they trying to do?"
To the world, the churches' attempt at music is nearly laughable. Attempting to witness through the tools of music, while simultaneously having no musical accountability, is one of the many asinine attempts of the church in 21st Century society. The dying world doesn't need a Christian branding or team-building exercise… The world needs our best representation of our hope in Christ that should be evident in all of our pursuits and presentations.

It isn't a foreign concept in our world to work toward goals in order to accomplish them. It is only in the church that this ignored and/or forgotten reality prevails on so many levels. Of course, the church needs to spend time removing the beam from its own eye before it runs outside to "fix" or "save" other people. A lot of the work that needs to be done begins with denouncing the lies the church has told itself about both themselves and the lost, and how great the differences between the two are. People are just people, and all of us need to come to grips with the Lord… and what he says about our tasks and how he expects us to get the job accomplished.

Our task cannot be accomplished as long as the eyes of the congregation are on the worship leader; or as long as the minds of the band members are focused on "not goofing up", as they try to make it through whatever tune is often being poorly presented! An invitation to the congregation cannot be realistically extended if the congregation is wincing in pain or embarrassment due to poor musical presentation. I've seen this sort of thing far too often… and you have, too! If *"God don't make junk"* we might do well to re-think what's happening on the platform before the funny and insightful pastor hits the stage! Worshiping musicians have a very important job to do before the pastor sweeps in to present the Word of God!

All About The Heart…
A person's presence on a worship team isn't completely about their "heart"! This misguided corporate church concept of this

bizarre statement as a be-all-end-all statement must meet its demise here and now. So, let's squash that tired, old and completely false lie before going forward. Is it dead? Yes? Thank you.

If you, as a worship leader, would rather have a group of total musical half-wits on your worship team… bless you, and please continue to do that. However, as a favor, please also stop showing-up to perform where the world can hear you? Thank you. They're already laughing. I'm just talking about one of the many reasons why they're laughing at the church. Since they're laughing (and they do laugh, when the music sucks), they can't hear what we're supposed to stand for, or what we're trying to say through the muddle and din of bad music! Even if the church has convinced itself that quality and ability do not matter… The world has not bought into the lie. When did the world begin holding the church to the concept of accountability? Interesting.

The allegedly wonderful hearts of all worship team leaders and participants are connected to their hands and minds, and the corresponding music speaks far more loudly to the state of their hearts than some show of piety or humility while performing the latest edition of the Christian Top 20.

Poor musical presentation, usually from the loudest and most visible player, is a guarantee that the same cloth-eared and tone-deaf player knows very little of the Lord's Word, their job, and even less about what their calling entails. I'm speaking from experience here. In addition to musical education, there should be a wealth of Biblical understanding and education – and absolutely not one instead of the other. Biblical understanding doesn't magically produce great musicians. It never has, nor will it ever do so.

But, let's not completely throw out the baby with the bathwater over this heart thing…

True, the heart of the individual is important. Albeit in a completely different way than the church forces that particular issue. The said "great heart" isn't important on any sort of quantifiable level when it comes to the musical job worship musicians are to perform. What about the actual task the musician is to perform? You know, the musical task! What about the task of presenting MUSIC through undeniable performance. What about "the job"? "Great hearts" don't produce great music. But, honestly, who truly has a great heart? I have (and you have too) witnessed a worship team participant or leader that is so in the way of the worship presentation that they actually impair the congregational worship experience! What about those situations when a person is playing or singing so poorly (or acting so unruly) as to even prevent worship? We've all been there, too!

This situation is largely exampled by participants who don't fully understand their job as a worship leader, or team participant. Which speaks beyond the player to a worship pastor who also doesn't understand their job anymore than the job of those persons he/she is supposed to be leading!

Quite honestly, I've had to quietly remove myself from a sanctuary on more than one occasion to rid myself of some Sunday morning random act of distracting, quasi-spiritual musical terrorism.

That isn't a sin, by the way, (that is) to leave the sanctuary. Gutting-it-out through bad music doesn't make anyone a 'better' Christian. Removing yourself is simply honesty in action. Leaving is fine. Just don't scream,

"What the *()&%$#@ is wrong with you people?!? Are you all deaf?! I'm tearing out my eardrums with a spork, and everyone is ignoring this horrible assault on our ears!! Is it just me?!"

Okay… that would be sin. But, allowing Granny Nanny Funklebanny's embarrassing and assaulting rendition of any tune, "sacred" or "secular" isn't what we sign-up for when we join a church. Let's always laugh together, cry together, hope together, live together, and love one another. As importantly, let's strive to be the people we're called to be and hold one another accountable in love. If this is "family business", then let's eliminate the matter seriously and remove the obnoxious insincerity and hackneyed attempts at musical worship. If you're not musically gifted… sit down. Please? The Lord will fill that spot on the team with an able body, if we allow him the time he's going to take doing so!

As a member of Christ's body I'm asking, "can we get it together?" Can we admonish one another in truth and toward the Lord's mandates and precepts? If nothing else, I'm hoping this book is a humorous addition to those other Christian books that line your shelves. You and I both know there are readers using this book to start their fireplaces after the "Granny Nanny Funklebanny" thing! Fine. I've said nothing heretical. Though I may have more than a slight irreverence toward some of the pharisaic traditions in the church in this area of music and there is truth even in the controversy of how I'm saying what needs to be said. Honestly, given my choices, I'd rather play with musicians like myself than be called to help deal with this necessary change in the church. It's far easier to ignore the crappy silliness and simply not participate. But, here we are.

Back to this "heart" thing…

Have you ever asked yourself the question, "Why is that person playing on the worship team?" Particularly if the person obviously should never (ever) play in public? The question is, "to whom, and what, are they 'ministering'?" When did the unnecessary game of musical Russian roulette become such a familiar (if not dreaded) part of our weekly congregational observance?

The statement I'm making is not about judgment as much as it is about truth - as much as it smacks of common sense and some level of compassion, even if it lacks tact! Sometimes, truth transcends tact. Particularly, if truth is being altogether ignored by, or being rebelled against by the listener. Then again, there is often more grace given in church than common sense and reason on a regular basis, isn't there? Tolerating the insidious is only putting the church further to sleep and further out of step with God's Word. Someone should ask some of the questions I'm asking in these pages. So, I'm asking…

As the church we should be standing at the pinnacle of meaningful expression and exacting execution of music. Instead, we have a great deal of pretending going on in the church – particularly (again) in the area of music.

For instance, the appearance of piety or churchliness shouldn't be the standard by which any worship team participant is invited onto the platform – whether that person "looks adequately worshipful, or humble", or not. If the church is going to insist upon using music, then, that music should be incredibly well presented. There. I said it.

The response by the worship leader to questions about the presence of a particular person who plays poorly Sunday after Sunday typically sounds something like,

"Weeell, brother Zemundikus (is that a real name? I hope not) *isn't the best kazoo player. But he sure has a grrrreeeeat heart! Just a super guy! He loooves to play it loud, and he insists on joining the team every Sunday! He can't ever make practice. I guess he does 'prayer nap' on Wednesday nights. I dunno… But, he's a worshiper! You should meet him, 'cause he looooves musicians like yourself. He came to my house when Horace, my pet manatee, fell ill, back a few years ago… Oh, and he makes great cookies for the children in the toddler ministry!"*

I openly challenge that inane thought process – even if my humor is a little warped! If a person doesn't understand their role and responsibility on the worship team, what constitutes a "great heart" in the specific area of the task they're supposed to perform? We are talking about music, right? Were we discussing cookies? Really?! When I've attempted to get the commentator back on track about music, I'm usually met with either blank stares or I'm asked,

"Why don't you think Brother Zemundikus should be there? Where is your heart?! He has been a part of this church for 30 years… back when there were 200 people here every Sunday!"

Ephesians 5:15

"Be very careful, then, how you live—not as unwise but as wise, making the most of every opportunity, because the days are evil. Therefore do not be foolish, but understand what the Lord's will is." [Emphasis added]

We need to reconsider who is doing what… and why - particularly in the area of those most public and visible areas of church leadership or Christian witness. We also need to understand what, exactly, constitutes a "great heart" and how that fact is manifested musically, in addition to spiritually, when speaking about church leadership, music and musicality. I also contend that if a person who insists upon playing music poorly as a member of a worship team may not possess this mythical great heart in the first place. **Jeremiah 17:9** speaks well to the heart of this errant church player, as well as to the hearts of those who justify this weird behavior, when it plainly says, *"The heart is deceitful above all things and beyond*

cure. Who can understand it?"
That is potentially all of us, in any situation, as we are representatives of Christ wherever we go. The church lavishly lays the "good heart" tag on those who refuse to work hard to do what we've been called to do on a level beyond the average church player on the average worship team. Once again, I must identify

this attitude as being completely counter to the one we should have about our witness inside the church walls and in the fallen world we live in.

Chapter 4

The following is another example of the upside down thinking in the average church.

Watch Me Worship...

In this "post-Christian" or "post-Church" age we are now living in, the concept of using music as a tool has become little more than a platform for the obviously visible worship leader types to play an interesting game I like to call "watch me worship". The game of "WMW" is really interesting to witness.

The "worship leader" is very often someone who generally isn't musical, as most of us understand musical ability, per se. So, that being identified as the chief problem...

The worship leader is followed by a group of band participants who also aren't particularly musically accountable, or able, and who can do little more than barely hanging onto the song they're attempting to present/play/perform. As whatever musical cacophony limps along, the leader weeps; looks dreamily into the ceiling (Heaven) while pounding his/her chest, and pleads with

Heaven to manifest the miracle of turning poorly played (and often awful sounding) music into something useable by God. Not only that... But, what a *performance* by the ever-humble (and just) worship leader! Yet, good music played well in the church is viewed negatively as 'performance' by the average Christian in America. Interesting. I've actually met Christians who have trouble worshiping to well played and well presented worship music in a live context!

Are most Christians so accustomed to awful music that they are shocked when the music is well done? Is that why most worship music played in the average church is so badly presented? That isn't to say that God can't use poorly played music. But, that isn't the point either, is it?

Worship Leaders (generally speaking, let alone the average church player) have no idea that their job may entail preparing the called players on their given team(s) for something greater than their shoddy rendition of some often badly written song that simply mentions Jesus' wonderful Name often enough to make the song a "Christian song". Does the average worship leader actually know who the called players on their team are? How are they encouraging and teaching these musicians beyond asking them to play every weekend and telling them "you're so great", so they'll stick around?

Here is a question I often ask in church circles, "have you ever noticed that the title *'Worship Pastor/Leader'* typically conjures thoughts of a person who isn't a particularly well-rounded musician, nor do they actually pastor the group of church players they've been given to 'lead'?"

Honestly, in this day and age, the average worship pastor serves as little more purpose than a stage personality or cheerleader. Certainly the title "cheerleader" rings more true than they are men or women who drive, or enliven, the particular musical vision of the fellowship that employs them. That is to imply that the church they're working for has an actual vision for the worship program beyond the typical "let's show up and see what happens!" type of loose weirdness I've seen over the past decades.

Instead of building great players who truly worship through their chosen instrument, the worship leader/pastor usually very cunningly convinces their team that *"less is more"*, or *"let's play it exactly like the recording"* as a rouse to never build actual worshiping, or musically able, musicians. Or, more so, this is a statement of their complete lack of trust in their players' ability to present the song in a true (much less original) fashion! As a result, most people who participate on worship teams have no idea that the actual job isn't about jangling semi-musically in the shadow of some wing-nut who should be doing most of what he or she is doing in front of the congregation in their own home… and in private!

Leading worship is for the congregation. It is not for the worship leader, and it's not for the worship team participants! The worship leader's job is to lead (nurture, teach, fellowship, etc) and prepare the team who are to lead the sheep! So… lead them! Instruct them, and raise able musicians who can be trusted to interpret the music realistically and actually. Don't give the players or the congregation the same lesson in "how to worship like me" every Sunday.

Of course, the idea of how to worship changes (again) once the cool moves from the next worship concert media for home viewing is released, devoured, and presented to the congregation as an original concept by the "genius" worship leader!

Christians are so afraid that great musical ability somehow equals musical performance! Meanwhile, the worship leader is breathlessly pantomiming and drawing all the attention in the room… to them! That's performance! And it's too often bad performance, by-and-large. Especially when you later see the same sweaty, crying person who 'led' worship at the local after-church eatery and hear him or her say, "yeah, I really wasn't into it today…" to their clique of all-too-willing and ever-present worship leader/worship music worshiping sycophants. I've also personally witnessed the sharp demeanor change while talking with a local worship leader/celebrity in a grocery store, when one of their avid fans joins our previously private conversation. Yeah, that's another one of those "too often to count" scenarios.

As far as the young up-and-coming church players are concerned… They should be encouraged to continue learning and growing as actual musicians – even beyond the worship leader or local fellowship. Not as the Lord demands… but as I speak. That's a joke. Let's see what happens with that statement!

Unfortunately, for the most part, once these musical sophomores (at best) reach the 'main stage' of their local church, they feel they've "arrived", and almost never continue to learn what it means to be a true musician. This is because the average church is a great place to hang out if your ego needs a good stroking! With a minimal amount of common, unpolished musical talent you, too, can become the self-professed coolest thing since sliced bread! You'll hear how great you are (just for showing up, mostly) every week.

This is another great disservice of the church to lieutenant musicians, and this is why some of the worst wannabes in any town are those players who can't actually play music, but continue to hear how wonderful they are at their home church. The thought and attitude of "why grow?" is rampant in the musical environment of the average church.

Integrity and accountability are out the window, and no one is leading anyone anywhere or to do anything beyond the secluded importance of the inward looking home fellowship. This sounds like the greatest recipe for failure ever foisted upon ignorant and lazy people. A perfect storm of complacency, if you will, and one of the dirtiest tricks the devil ever pulled is manifested in this fact on a weekly basis. What could the average worship leader do with a group of very musically able and Biblically agile worshiping musicians? The fact that such an environment scarcely exists is one of the greatest tragedies of the church in the 21st Century.

Chapter 5

The Christian Music Industry is like this...

Christian music has become more of an "industry" and a means of "Christian entertainment" that has in turn become most often employed to separate the average Christian person from those naughty, vile, and sub-culturally unacceptable pop artists, rappers, and spotlight grubbing peddlers of sexual filth that pervade our radio waves and television screens. YIKES! Who wouldn't want to be saved from that, and brought into the loving arms of the local, regional, or national Christian community?

The "Christian Music industry" began in earnest in the 1970s as an alternative to the spandex-and bustier-clad invasion of (what was and would become) music television and its predecessor, concert music television. Anyone remember shows like The Midnight Special and Don Kirchner's Rock Concert? Great shows! Fair enough.

Back to Christian music as an industry…

The downfall of any 'industry" is the fact that it soon becomes much more about promoting and selling product than about the dissatisfaction, or lack of viable product that originally began the movement.

The Christian popular music movement began with what appeared to be honest, truehearted young men and women who wanted to rock! But they wanted to rock for, and in the name of, Jesus. The pioneers of what became this now overblown, showy, too often dishonest, far too often slimy if not musically sub-par subculture were simply artists and bands who may have also sought something not unlike "fame" for the sake of Christ's Kingdom… and for themselves. This sounds very human, and I've never met a person on earth who wasn't completely human. So, there should be no shock or surprise in this statement.

All that to make this particular point: at the 40-year mark of this industry, Christian music has made the unnecessary point of being musically separate and, as a result, has failed to remain even vaguely relevant or equal to the musical and music production advancements of actual, earthbound music and its industry.

True, artists who also happen to be people of faith occasionally release a wonderful musical statement of worship-based material. Which, by-the –way, is generally openly accepted and often acclaimed by music lovers of any spiritual status, because the music and production is top notch. But, that product isn't part of the Christian music industry I'm talking about!

Music made by young Christian musicians and producers in the secular arena, when compared to the general product of the Christian music industry, are often two very different (and as often musically contradicting) entities.

At least that was by and large the case before the general demise of the record label as we previously understood them, beginning in earlier this century! Thankfully, many great artists and bands are growing product from home, and the primary learning curve lies in production value more so than some overblown, corporate entity that is simply in the business of duplicating itself and its product ad infinitum. There are many great singer-songwriters, who also happen to be Christians, who are releasing viable music and who display enviable production skills! But, those aren't the artists who will ever be played by the "Christian Brand" radio stations that make a further mockery of the genre by only playing music produced before 1997.

Can we agree that much of the music released by the Christian music industry lacks the sheen and finish of the average product offered by the secular community - whether recorded by professional musicians, Christian or not? When looked at from that place of sincerity and simplicity, is it any wonder that secular music offers a musically alluring component that is absent in much of today's Christian music? That allure is often far more musical than anything that lies in the lyrical content of a given song. That is to say, from the standpoint of musical quality.

Since we're discussing the matter, we should come to terms with the fact that the world doesn't necessarily view the Christian music industry as a sort of musical joke (by-and-large) because the world, as a people group, is actively rejecting Jesus more and more every day. On the contrary, the world more often than we (the "Big 'C' Church" care to believe) has rejected the words of Jesus based upon the actions of His people and the strange and poor view they believe us to have about the arts and, in particular, music. It isn't because of some Victorian rejection of nudity or dance music that Christian music is generally poorly played and/or produced! It is simply because much of Christian music… sucks.

As much as Christian music generally lacks a deeper production and musical value, it may be the case that Christian producers and artists seem to be engrossed in some futile attempt to make the music sound holy, instead of simply making great sounding and well played music! This is more of that Christian branding thing I've been talking about. For instance, I've heard the same, lame programmed drum sequence turn up in 3 of the top 5 Christian songs very recently! That beat was pedestrian at best the first time I heard it. But, here it is again on another Christian brand artist's top single! It's as if the Christian industry has taken a concept by another genre and made it… sillier! By "sillier" I mean: removing all apparently threatening ethnicity from the song's barely evident groove, so that the homogeneous subculture of Christian listeners aren't tainted by a desire to dance! In other words, "let's use hip-hop, and other ethnic facets of music… but let's wring all that stuff out of the music!" Great idea, he joked!

It often sounds like the music of the Christian industry is being governed and overseen by people who are wholly out of touch with anyone or any music beyond itself, as if it was conceived and produced in a vacuum of some mythical Mayberryesque laboratory where no one actually lives! Most Christians I know don't even live there! Again, there are a few (very few) Christian artists who have actual musical depth and worth, and when you finally hear them you almost immediately understand that their music is what they would produce regardless of the existence of a Christian music industry! Those true artists are also the ones who are the most genuine and who truly live the music they're given to create. Meanwhile, many of the Christian industry artists I've met (and/or worked for) act as much the Prima Donna; as much the misunderstood or misguided, shuffling rock star, or suffering artist, and as much the celebrated personality as anyone I have met (and worked for) in the realm of secular music!

The primary difference in my experience has always been the fact that secular music pays far better; it typically sounds more genuine, and it is simply more enjoyable to play. Never underestimate the old adage, "you get what you pay for."

By contrast, Christian industry artists are far too busy attempting to appear holy or sound anointed, in a commercial sense, instead of happily being the musical entities they were created to be.

If anything, the world generally views Christian music as "safe". By that I mean unobtrusive and innocuous. It's "easy listening" at best! Particularly once you've made up your mind about this Jesus character, and there is no further compulsion toward the wonder of life, its origin, or it creator.

It is apparent to the listening non-Christian that the idea of the squeaky-clean Christian music artist is as much a farce as the squeaky-clean born again worker in any office or workaday atmosphere. So, why is the industry so determined to sell this whacked out, and completely out of touch, image?

Life happens outside the vacuum and sooner or later (generally sooner) every person's true colors come forth in the daily environment. O how the mighty have fallen, everywhere people are smashed together in society! Instead of being a viable witness to the doomed office workers surrounding the "Christian Brand" employee, Christian music may have become the soundtrack of that crazy, backbiting, gossiping weirdo who claims grace while eyeing their co-workers with damning contempt and contrived pity that everyone besides them is going to hell.

Christian music will only have as much worth to the unbeliever as the Christian they most often deal with in their daily lives. So, is Christian music solely for the purpose of Christian entertainment? Or, is it a witness to the world? Is it both? Or is it actually neither? Or, is it simply a type (or genre) of music and very little more than that? There are people who wear only "this" type of blue jeans, and others who would rather fight than put "that" brand on their body. Right? Maybe the world looks at the Christian Brand as nothing more than that. Choice. It certainly seems so to me. I'm not sure the "ministry" should be about teaching people "how to appear", instead of the much more time consuming concept of teaching people "who to be".

Perhaps the failure of the Christian church and much of Christian music lies in the thought that we were never supposed to separate Christian music from the ones who most need it, and those of us called to present it, in the first place! What if the Lord enjoys some of the music Christians reject as "unacceptable", every day? Can you honestly say the Lord didn't make Pat Metheny, "Pat Metheny"? Have you ever heard his music? How about Prince? Are you truly convinced the Lord didn't really mean that – regardless of his spirituality?

It also strikes me as completely contradictory to our witness that most musician converts to Christianity weren't witnessed to or loved into the Kingdom by anyone from the Christian music industry! The fact is, Christians who also happened to work in the secular music industry, most likely, originally witnessed to the runaway majority of celebrity musician converts I've met! I'm yet to hear, "I was trying to find Jesus, and (enter name of well-known Christian artist or industry head) called me to talk about their Savior!"

Notice I'm not talking about Christian radio that teaches God's Word to whomever happens to dial in! I'm working hard to completely debunk the separation of Christian music from secular society – as much as Christians aren't supposed to be living outside of the world we've been sent into for the purpose of being "little Christs".

When did Christians become so unnecessarily afraid of the world we live in, as if we were afraid of being infected by it?

That same fear produces the same 'married for decades' folks who've never walked through The Song of Solomon with their spouse. God made sex and told us where, when and how to do it correctly. Right? He speaks plainly about all aspects of our human lives in His Word! Without the foundation of how we are to live before the world, how can we truly witness anything to anyone? I digress.

Christ in his word has much to say about music, and how we're to present it, and even who is supposed to present it – as leaders in the local fellowship!

These things I'm saying about music, the church, and a necessary revolution in the Christian's attitude toward their given mission, aren't completely 'new' concepts! Yet, it is apparent that many of these ideas are daily ignored by he average Christian as they pursue something other than the call to excellence from the Holy Spirit, and the cross (hard work) we're called to bear each day.

We are all completely fallen, and we are never holy as a human entity without Christ. Therefore, we must realize how powerful music is, and how using it badly has created a deeply troubling response by the unbeliever to the One True God. Along with that, we may need to realize that it is largely our fault that this has happened! Only God is good, and much of our Christian popular music attempts are little more than fallen humans stumbling about in Pharisee's clothing in some crazy attempt to make "our" music worthy of His Name, instead of being the musicians who can freely witness Christ's love in us and through us as our abilities scream in favor of a living and loving Lord!

What if the Lord doesn't need our lame attempts to create "a place for us", and what if we are sinning by doing little more than idolizing our equally fallen Christian industry personalities, as much as the world idolizes their own musical performers? Music isn't magic! That is, unless you've simply never bothered to learn what music is and how it should be used…

Chapter 6

Musicians are like this…
Most life-long musicians I know intimately often find themselves deeply touched by songs and musical expression, and they tend to live in a realm that allows their heart to remain in search of something I call the "deep dance of the soul". This particular

lifestyle is a necessary part of their musical practice.

Throughout the years I've also met other types of artists, music hobbyists, and music appreciators that share a similar practice - whether or not they are actual musicians has little to do with their practice of listening and worshiping the Lord through a personal music experience. Likewise, most life-long Christian professional musicians I know couple this search with the desire to worship and "dance like David", unabashedly and without care of who's watching, to whatever song is prompting the dance! Humorously, we're also often despised for doing exactly that by the church – who, for some reason, insists that visceral expression is contrary to what we were made to do. Shameful.

By contrast, I love watching my dear Christian Brother and bassist Abraham Laboriel! Abe is going to worship regardless of who he's playing music with, or playing for! All the music he plays is for his savior and Lord Jesus Christ, and he is completely unrepentant in his musical presentation and display of worship! That said, Abe has also enjoyed a long and fruitful career as a session and live musician who plays across many musical genres. He is just one of the many strong believers working in both Christian and secular music, and his witness for Christ lies in his musical ability and in his beautiful personality. His faith speaks loudly in how he does, what he does… and for whom he does it. Check out Abe with Ron

Kenolly and other professional Christian worship environments. Also, check him out with Larry Carlton, Go West, and a host of others! He dances like David, and it is completely and joyfully infectious! Thank you, Abraham, for your friendship, leadership and undying devotion to our Lord, and to your art! Our discussions on the topic of music have ministered deeply to my soul.

If you can identify yourself as a "church player" research and find those dozens of Christian musicians who work in the secular community to learn what it means to be an effective witness for Christ though music. In each case, musical witness starts with being an incredible musician who is beyond "blessed" or "talented".

I mentioned dancing earlier, and the air reverberated with negative responses like:

"Isn't dancing for brown people and infidels?"

"See? I told you he would start talking about that 'y'all can't dance', thing! That's why this book is wrong!"

"God don't like no dancin'! He says so right there in Paul's first book to them Saspirillos!"

"Off with his head!"

Just Joking. Sort of…

The idea here is to understand how differently musicians process the learning and expression of music than the average person, and certainly differently than those average church players previously identified. I would honestly disagree that a person "becomes" a musician as much as they learn to "be" the musician they are through their life practices, and that practice is as deeply musical as it is spiritual. To that point, I don't believe once a person identifies themselves as a musician that the matter is something that can be turned on or off when the same person is in church, at the grocery store, or in the dentist's chair. As far as being a musician is concerned, you either are… or, you are not. It isn't a matter of "when", or in what context we're discussing.

Musicians are often about the business of music and, as an end-result, songs. It is amazing how often the songs in question are not Christian songs, even when discussing songs with a Christian musician. It is also amazing how often the same is true for the more adept worship leaders I've met!

Every musician I know has a heart's soundtrack, and with those musician-friends I am most intimate with, I can merely ask, "what's playing?" in their soul, to completely understand their heart. If I can hear the song that's playing in my friend's heart… I understand a lot about what they are feeling and thinking, and how their life is moving though the process of praise and of life's challenges.

If this concept seems weird to you… you're probably not a musician – even if you participate on your church's worship team. That's an honest statement. That isn't to say that if you have an identifiable heart's soundtrack, you are a musician. But, if it is the case that you posses a soundtrack that is dear to you, you're probably more artistic or musical than many people on the planet!

So the question is, what are you doing with the music that so deeply lives within you? As I said earlier, I identify this idea as a means of identifying how differently a musician processes their world. I am also stating these things so the average worship leader (who is typically not a musician, in the truest sense) can understand what they're dealing with when they approach true musicians. Or, more so, why worship leaders have such difficulties dealing with individuals who posses a musical soul they, themselves, often do not posses.

As much as the 'position' of worship team member should not be sought by the unmusical, worship leaders should not be people who cannot lead musically in knowledge, ability, and calling. Of the many worship leaders I've met, very few have a real working relationship with music and even fewer have a heart soundtrack that allows them to relate to others from a musical standpoint.

As I've said, the wonderful thing about the heart of musicians and the songs they deeply love and worship to, is the fact that whether a particular tune is considered "secular" or "sacred" is passé at best in the matter of what the song says to them! In most cases, the song isn't a "Christian song" regularly living in the heart many of the musicians I regularly pray with. That is not to say that Christian songs are largely rejected, as much as it is to say that true musicians see the Lord's glory in all of music, and it's our relationship with the music we've worshiped to in our lives that speaks directly to the songs we're playing today.

More profoundly, it's the knowledge of the music that's come before a given day's musical event that constitutes the musical ability I'm blathering on-and-on about. The content of the song in our musical history speaks deeply into whatever song we're currently playing – regardless of that song's spiritual context. So, in essence, if there's nothing in a player's musical well… they have nothing with which to grow today's musical crop. Many church players have a dry well, and if there's nothing in there to begin with… nothing is coming out of there for themselves, or for the sake of others!

Honestly, most Christians I know don't rehearse and recite

Christian songs regularly! Especially if we're discussing music outside of the church walls! This humorous fact speaks volumes to me as it pertains to this subject! For many God-fearing Christian people, it isn't unusual for a song that has nothing to do with the church, or Christ, and/or often performed by persons who may be very far from God (in the typical Evangelical sense of the term) to regularly turn their worship toward our Heavenly Father! Though this is an easily understood phenomenon, many church people make an ignorant association between 'secular songs' and carnality.

Can the Lord use any song He chooses to reach into our hearts? What about the hearts of the unsaved? Why isn't it okay to relate a secular song to the Christian song we're playing during the sacred worship service? Music is music… and music is very powerful! Period. Regardless if it is played well, or played poorly (in false piety), music will always make a deep impression on the listener. This fact speaks volumes to my point!

Can those poor, lost, unwitting, pro-wife-swapping-baby-shaking weirdoes - wearing the headbands and chrysanthemum outfits - really be used of God Almighty to reach someone, through true musicality? Should we good people allow such an unchristian thing to happen inside our own dear hearts? Should we frozen chosen wear T-shirts that say, "NO Groove on MY Watch" to prove our holiness, while trying desperately to undo music in ourselves and in others?

Considering this idea I need to ask the question, "does God simply like music?" Does God like all types of music? Did His creation have stipulations about music? Or, is music simply something He created for His pleasure, and ours, and for our use? Of course, I'm not talking about music that is used to rage and war against Christ. But, how about music that is neither "for" nor "against" Christ? What does the Lord say about songs written about love, pets, daytime, food, or weather conditions? Does all good music lean toward praising the Lord if we are believers?

Meteorologist understand what types of clouds are in the sky, and they may even understand how the clouds are created, how quickly they're traveling, and the types of weather they're associated with. But, they may not necessarily know the God of all – Who is the maker of wind, weather and cloud. Obviously, knowing the weather isn't worship any more than knowing how to grunt lyrics or grimace musically prevents or allows God to use song to reach souls in need of his gently ministering hand.

This is a great place to mention that one of the greatest ministry tools in the hand of a particular band I played in was our rendition of the Beatles' "Eleanor Rigby". Believe it, or not, that song represents the first time I thought about the hereafter. I was four years old. That song still ministers very deeply to me. So, you see, songs minister…

God can use, and has used, 'secular' songs to reach into the lives of thousands of people for His Glory, because He is not limited (or impressed) by our attempt at musical worthiness! As far as the gift of music is concerned, he gives gifts to all people – regardless if those people choose to use those gifts for his sake and purposes, or not. God can and does use whatever he wants to use at any time. Even the weather! Right? Is it something unusual or extraordinary for the Lord to use music, any music, to reach the musical or particularly musically inclined?

The Lord has given us various commands and laws to help us understand our lives, spouses, children, and the world we live in… Whether we follow them, or not, isn't the point. God gave his commandments along with the gifts he gave to humankind! He wrote a book about how we should live and how we should present our witness before an unbelieving world. We must choose to learn about this if we are to be called people of God, who are called for his purpose.

My point about the meteorologist has to do with the fact that weather is based upon real theories and concepts. The people who understand these principles are called meteorologists, or "weather experts". If meteorologists learn to understand the technical aspects of weather and not the God Who made the weather… it almost seems like a waste of worship (or purpose), doesn't it? Because it is so evident that the Lord is speaking to people through the blessings and warnings inherent in weather and climate!

If this understanding holds true, then it isn't a stretch to understand that music, painting, sculpting, architecture, dance, comedic timing and graphic art are also God breathed gifts to mankind, and that he speaks through these things to us. He also gives us warnings about how to use these arts.

Back to music… Learning the rules of music is neither sacred nor secular. If the theory is already there, why don't more worship pastors and church players use it to reach others for His sake? Would we better understand what the Lord has already said about the matter of music, through study? When did the idea of study become so abhorrent to the church? Honestly, would you get your weather from a person with a "grrreat heart'" but who never looks out their window?

The rules of music are no less invaluable than understanding traffic rules before you drive out of your driveway and into traffic! Humorously (more so unfortunately), it is the average church player who doesn't know anything about the music they're attempting to use to praise the Lord through song! Yet, these are the same people who will attempt to tell anyone who will listen that they are talented and that people should come hear them play… at their church, where no one else understands music either, and where poorly played music has so much become the norm that well played music is looked upon as a super power! The painful truth is that the average church player believes if they say the Name of Jesus enough it'll somehow create good music. Where is the teaching worship pastor in the midst of this mess?

I understand that by inviting a person to their church the church player's attempt may be to introduce someone to the Lord they claim to serve. At least, this is true as an initial hope and attempt. But, what if they and their group present awful music to the people they invite to their church? Should Jesus fix the issue? Or, should the church player initially understand their calling so that the people they invite to their church can more effectively meet Jesus – potentially through the player's hard work, discipline, and understanding of an art-form that can draw strangers into the church? Or, could their evident lack of knowledge (and poorly played music) actually act as a repellent to the people they invite to their fellowship? I know I've been personally repelled by a church's music long before I heard the pastor preach the message!

So, why does the average church player feel they should strike out on some unnecessary 'path of musical discovery' to play Almighty God's music, instead of simply becoming an actual student of music? Why are there "schools of worship" that completely ignore the idea of teaching music to their students? Some schools in operation today teach the look and actions of false piety instead of teaching anything that has to do with music. As if "Christian" is a brand to aspire to. Pity. Why are Christians pouring resources into worship schools that prepare their students for little more than appearing pious or humble through the use of music?

Does the Lord require a musical genre, or musically oriented brand, that is dedicated (at least in word, if not in deed) to himself? Or is this really about how music makes us feel, and how to attempt to manipulate it – rather than understand it? Simply put, worshiping the Lord doesn't create good music in and of itself. It appears that smart, secular culture following church marketing trend experts have decided that our faith should be more about a brand (or appearance) than substance, and little more beyond that. Look around… This isn't myth, or doomspeak!

One of the reasons the church has become so grossly ineffective is because of its lack of focus on the jobs we've been given, equipped for and called to perform. The church has become so "politically correct" that it has fooled itself into believing in no mission at all. Without a mission, there is no accountability, no credibility, and no consequences for failing. Everyone seems to be so busy showing up (at least, for the cool, visible assignments) that no one knows how to accomplish the objective of the sought after and hard won position! The mentality is, "it doesn't matter what you do for the church, as long as you show up to do... something!"

YAY! Welcome to failure!

How many of you think I'm bashing the church right now? How many of you know your job, and know how to become fully equipped to accomplish your job in Christ? Last question: how many of you understand that grace doesn't do your job for you?

Like many parents, I challenge my children to be the absolute best they can be. I help my children get the proper coaching and tutoring for their sport and academic struggles respectively, and I make certain that they have a chance at excellence in those things that interest them. Like many parents, the Lord has most likely placed you in an environment that gives you every opportunity to find a great music teacher who can help you achieve your musical goals – just as he's placed you in a church that hopefully directs you toward understanding his Word as deeply and fully as you're mentally capable of doing. The question is: why aren't you in lessons to become a better musician and/or vocalist if you're insisting that you're called to reach the world (your church, your neighbor, your cat) for Christ through music?

I have to be honest with you and tell you that I've never had a problem witnessing to people about how great Jesus is to me. Not because I'm comfortable with the idea of chatting with strangers about Christ. I'm not. But, because my mission field is most often the audience who is listening to one of the artists or bands I work with. Most often, witnessing begins with someone offering praise concerning my musical ability either during a set break, or after I've played. The first response, of course, is "thank you!" But, about 15 years ago, I began adding, "playing well is only my reasonable act of worship to Christ." The listener's response is usually pretty funny! "Wha…?"

I then explain that being the best musician I can be, regardless of where the gig takes me, is an opportunity for me to give back hours of practice (something I own) to the Lord as worship. After all, he gave me the ability to want to learn to play well and to be a player who makes listeners happy with the music I've been given to pursue and to make for Christ's sake. The conversation doesn't take very long, and often the appreciative listener simply smiles and takes their leave. Sometimes, however, my response to their compliments leads to lengthy and in-depth discussions about my talents and how that relates to the goodness of God. I really like those times! It has never happened that a person has reacted poorly to my witness. Never. That's because regardless if they think I'm bonkers for worshiping Christ, or not... I play well, and they enjoyed what I had to say musically. I'm not sure my job description goes much further than that, honestly!

Christian professional musicians, regardless of the musical genre they most often participate in, worship the Lord. Period. All music played by the Christian musician will present an element of worship within it. That's _all_ music, and not just worship music, or Christian music.

In so saying, perhaps certain secular music genre and musical artists exist simply because the Lord loves music! All music! What a thought! Maybe the Lord wanted The Beatles... to be the Beatles. This is a way of thinking that generally escapes non-musical church people. But it is something the musician fully understands and greatly appreciates. I mention this group because I hear their influence in a wide variety of music, and in much of Christian music – even if the average Christian music listener ignores the fact. So, why listen to music that sounds like a particular group, instead of simply listening to the source?

Do most listeners of "CCM", "Gospel", and/or Christian "P&W" music in general honestly believe the music they're listening to has no 'secular' musical influences? Is music that speaks the name of Jesus 'holy', while music that doesn't mention Christ 'secular', and therefore unfit for the Christian individual?

This is a ridiculous thought, isn't it? Yet, I find many Christians thinking in this exact manner toward many "Christian artists", many of whom aren't original, profound, or even Christian – as we're witnessing more and more "Christian artists" who aren't even believers in Christ! Yet, the industry thrives – all the while making no promise that the person telling us, "Jesus is wonderful!" has anything to do with the work of Christ... anymore than the Beatles. After all, they sang about "love" a LOT, didn't they?

The Christian music industry is nothing more than a business. Not that the Lord cannot or doesn't use these individuals or this industry. He can do anything with anything! But, the idea of the church being so bound by titles concerns me. Food for thought, isn't it? Let's get back to the thought process of the average "church player" in the average church in Average America...
Eleanor Rigby (credited as Lennon-McCartney)

Recorded: April 28th, 1966 (Studio 2, Abbey Road Studios, London, England); April 29th, June 6th, 1966 (Studio 3, Abbey Road Studios, London, England)

Chapter 7

Correcting Worship Team Myths

This chapter is dedicated to debunking many of the myths surrounding music from the mouths of worship team leaders and participants I've worked with over the years.

"Being proficient on my instrument detracts from the Lord."

Colossians 1:16 says, *"All things were created by Him and for Him."*

So, not only did God give us the gift of music that he created for his glory, but he also puts "a new song" in our mouths (and hearts) – giving us new things to praise Him for. If God inhabits the praises of his people (Ps.22:3) and he has given us songs to praise him and to declare his worth. Then he has also given us music, good music and played well (I contend) to encourage and exhort one another in the Lord. How then, can we offer such poor music while simultaneously attempting to reach a dying world for the sake of our highly esteemed Lord and Savior? How does poorly done ever equal "good"? How are we to convince the world that Jesus is wonderful, if the music we're attributing to his name often isn't worth listening to?

The Bible fully supports the thought of giving our absolute all (musical and spiritual practice) so that God might use it to reach beyond the individual – instead of ignoring our call to excellence "for God's sake".

"I'm helping (the Lord) because I show up."

HMMM… I'm not really sure how to approach this one. By "showing up" without bothering to be musically and/ or spiritually prepared, the average church player is actually a musical liability to himself, the congregation, and to the musician visitor who may be in the congregation for that particular service. Imagine the called musician being musically prepared as an act of worship!

PLEASE STOP HELPING JESUS, and simply apply yourselves to the task of being what we claim to be: people of excellence who are called out of mediocrity by Almighty God. God's call is not about everyone else being excellent while you slide in the back door with your nonsense! We are to be used outside the church, too! Being called is about doing that thing within the church walls that you do in your every day life! If you're not a musician on the outside of the church walls… chances are you're not supposed to be pretending to be one inside the church! If you're a Christian and you're an awful musician… understand that your witness is about your poor skills, and you weaken the depth of your alleged relationship with Christ to others. In short, God doesn't suck! Why do your skills not speak to excellence? All actual Christian musicians should be in secular community as well as contributing to their church. Non-musicians should… knock it off! You can have a position when you've worked for it. There's nothing wrong with knowing who you are and understanding who you're not. Jesus knows every heart and the call he's placed on each of us, and he knows when we're too busy seeking position and beguiling ourselves into places we simply don't belong – both in the church and in the world.

"I'll never be a pro… But I really want to play at my church."

Is it a strange thought to begin a season of intense (ministry oriented) study BEFORE releasing oneself into the practice of an alleged ministry or calling? Why not set a goal to join a ministry team and seek a qualified music teacher in the meantime? Why did John baptize Jesus? Why did Jesus respond to his mother the way he did in John 2:4? There are tasks to fulfill and timing involved that is completely ignored by the average church player when answering the call to lead worship for the local fellowship. Timing and preparation are very important concepts to understand when looking at this aspect of Christ's life.

Was it that this was not the proper time for Jesus to perform attention-drawing miracles as yet, lest it should provoke his enemy Satan to seek his life before his time? Or, his meaning could have been that his time of doing miracles in public was not yet; and therefore, though he was willing to perform the miracle, he chose to do it in a very <u>private manner.</u> What was Jesus waiting for? Didn't his own brothers ask this same question concerning his actions? Was there timing involved that they didn't fully understand?

Now, how do we approach this idea as potential leaders in our fellowship? What can we learn by looking at the timing of Jesus public ministry? I have to say there was an absolute strategy and timing in everything Jesus did, and the idea is something for us to consider as we are released into our time of public demonstration of our personal calling.

"I'm working in the ministry via the worship team!"

Wrong. Before we go on, I should remind you that participating on a worship team is ***not*** an act of ministry! That is, not in the way in which one generally, or most often, thinks of the term *ministry*. Participating in any capacity before the congregation is, actually, **leadership**! *GASP* I know, right!? I've been saying this throughout the book.

So, then the church leadership should be very clear about those persons and personalities they're inviting to partner with them in any visible capacity – as they speak to the ideals and values of the church, often as loudly, or louder, than the pastor, elder board, or anyone else who is routinely less visible to the congregation. So, whatever the church leadership allows in the area of music speaks strongly to their viewed role in the church environment. Allowing poorly played music speaks loudly beyond the church walls and into the community that surrounds the church.

In order to lead properly, one should possess a grasp of the subject matter being discussed, and of the tools available to thoroughly example the point of the discussion. Therefore, worship team participation is leadership… Not ministry. And the leadership speaks volumes of the church's function. Have you ever noticed that people who have a deep background in accounting make great church accountants? Notice how that fact may, or not, speak to that particular person's "heart" in the church sense? Is the church accountant a minister more than they are, hopefully effectively, fulfilling a role they are designed for? I mean the enjoyment of spending money while possessing a working knowledge of mathematics is beyond the "great heart" of the matter, isn't it?

Its completely absurd to ignore a clear path winding through a dangerous and heavily forested area, and instead choose to go about clomping through the forest – even if 'keeping the path in sight' is part of the alleged plan. So, why aren't Christian worship team members taking it upon themselves to learn music theory, and why are so many hoping to blaze a heretofore-undiscovered musical path? You know, the path that isn't actually there? Why aren't Christian worship team members learning to play music at a very high level of proficiency? Why are worship pastors 'okay' with musical ignorance on the part of their team participants, and why aren't more worship pastors teaching music to their worship team? When did the church become so lazy, and why isn't anyone pointing this out?

Ministry through music is teaching a younger generation what it means to be a musician for the Lord – we cannot minister by being a musician in an active context. Exampling music, good or bad, isn't ministry in any way. Playing music is simply playing music; and attempting to achieve musical goals, or to teach musical credibility, through ignorance is not ministry in any way.

"Ministry" has become a general buzzword for service, and service cannot be achieved by pointing the congregation toward you, or to your worship leader.

Teaching music to Christian musicians is a ministry. But, first, you need to understand music theory, and you will also need to have a wealth of understanding about technique, tone, and time-feel as it pertains to music. In short, play well yourself, first!

Teaching someone how to appear worshipful is in no way

teaching them about music. More so than any other title (in church qualification) the church musician is actually an elder, or overseer…

1 Timothy 3:1 says, *"Here is a trustworthy saying: If anyone sets his heart on being an overseer, he desires a noble task."*

1 Tim 3:7 says, *"He must also have a good reputation with outsiders, so that he will not fall into disgrace and into the devil's trap."* [emphasis added]

What bigger trap exists for the church player than to never bother excelling in their craft, and to become a potential liability for true musicians, or music lovers? All the while there is applause and undue praise for the player who simply shows up to "play for Jesus" whether they're prepared, or not.

1 Tim 3:9-10 *says, "They must keep hold of the deep truths of the faith with a clear conscience. They must first be tested; and then if there is nothing against them, let them serve as deacons."* [emphasis added]

The church seems to have a sense of using the tool of music without truly being accountable to how, when, and by whom it should be used. More to the point… what is the job of the worship team and who is a true worshiper? I think answering those questions will also speak to the type of persons who are called to function in that particular capacity of church leadership in any fellowship.

The point I'm laboring to make is simply this: there is no secular or sacred in the way most people think about music, or about the learning of music! Music is music! It's either good music… Or, it isn't good. By good (of course) I mean well played, well presented, well produced and placed in a proper context. Good is good. Or… it isn't good. So, why isn't there more good music in the average church?

Who's Running This Show, Anyway…?

Is it truly risqué for a pastor to really enjoy any particular non-Christian musical artist or group? Would you leave the church pastored by an anointed and obviously called leader who is a Beatles fan? Well, what if like Spurgeon or Lewis, the pastor enjoys tobacco… even while studying the Word of God? Or, heaven forbid, one of the church leaders enjoys a glass of wine with his dinner? Have you ever heard this kind of comment, "well… the pastor knows the Word of God. But, I think he listens to hip-hop (or country. or metal. or reggae. or…) and that's weird!" If you've heard this, have you challenged the person who said this sort of thing?

Now, wait a minute... Let's not jump to conclusions of supposed excess, or anything hidden that I have not mentioned, or anything else I'm not saying. Yes. There are societal rules to consider, I suppose. But, we're not talking about that type of excess, are we? No. We're not.

The longer I hang around intelligent people, the more I find them to be absolutely average (moderate) in all the areas of their lives they are not completely passionate about, and I find most of them to be excessive and aggressive about those things they are passionate about. The conclusion is this: most of us have the idea that a certain thing should either be done well… or left alone. This is how I feel about music in the church. See? That isn't so hard to understand, is it?

The idea of what is sacred and what is secular speaks far more to an individual's religious bent than it does to their faith, and even more so than it speaks to the actual truth of a matter! By religious, I mean those precepts and concepts created by humankind in an attempt to make them more palatable to a Holy God. This attempt to make ourselves "holy by rules" simply doesn't work in any context. Let alone the strange (and often absurd) way we approach music in the church. So, what does it mean to deify worship music and the musicians who play it – while never understanding our God-assigned tasks enough to accomplish them?

Matthew 5:16: *"Let your light shine before men in such a way that they may see your good works, and glorify your Father who is in heaven."*

What would happen if we took the Lord at His Word in a way that pertains to the music this subculture called the church is making? What does this scripture mean, as it pertains to the church player's responsibility in the average church? The comparison isn't so positive when looked at through an actual clarity of vision, is it?

These are merely observations I've made over many years of experience. These observations also speak to the fact that most Christians' faux Victorian views about the church (the Bible is full of "you can't" and "you shouldn't" mentality) are no more true than the church's upside down view of how to deal with the arts community. Instead of building teams of people to do things, the church should spend far more time teaching and training its people about what it means to take on certain responsibilities and what the consequences are of accepting those responsibilities and then performing poorly due to ignorance, laziness, or rebellion. Luke 9:51-62 rings very true in this sense, doesn't it? Commitment doesn't equal arrival by any means.

So, why are so many church players complacent in their positions on worship teams, and why aren't worship pastors teaching the basic concepts of accountability, credibility, and musicality through the music these groups are attempting to make together?

Chapter 8

What is calling from a Biblical perspective?

Colossians 1:25-29

"I have become its servant by the commission God gave me to present to you the word of God in its fullness— the mystery that has been kept hidden for ages and generations, but is now disclosed to the Lord's people. To them God has chosen to make known among the Gentiles the glorious riches of this mystery, which is Christ in you, the hope of glory.

"He is the one we proclaim, admonishing and teaching everyone with all wisdom, so that we may present everyone fully mature in Christ. To this end I strenuously contend with all the energy Christ so powerfully works in me." New International Version (NIV) Bible [emphasis added]

The typical Evangelical Church's concept of understanding the tool of music and *how* and *why* they are using it in the first place has never been more ignored than at this particular time in history. Nor, is the ignored *how* and *why* in a more seemingly perilous situation, as in this present time, than any time past! Various reports would have you believe that fewer and fewer people call themselves "Christian", and even fewer have a correct understanding of what the term implies as a life mode. Yet, the church continues to ignore their nearly completely misunderstood use of God-given tools that were originally engineered to bring unbelievers (along with believers) into a place of worship.

Ephesians 5:15-20

"Be very careful, then, how you live—not as unwise but as wise, making the most of every opportunity, because the days are evil. Therefore do not be foolish, but understand what the Lord's will is. Do not get drunk on wine, which leads to debauchery. Instead, be filled with the Spirit, speaking to one another with psalms, hymns, and songs from the Spirit. Sing and make music from your heart to the Lord, always giving thanks to God the Father for everything, in the name of our Lord Jesus Christ."

New International Version (NIV) Bible [emphasis added]

WOW! How tragically the church has descended to a place that reeks of apathy and self-indulgent, second rate… almost everything! Have we truly ignored discipline so long that when we see it in others we so overtly hate it? Tragic.

"Be careful how you live"… Could we say, "be careful what you do; how you do it, and why you do it"?

Could we say, "how you play… where you play"?

How are we, "making the most of every opportunity" when every time a lost person enters a church, they see little more than this idea of, "It's all for Jesus, and Jesus doesn't mind if it sucks"!

Or, that it simply doesn't add up to God's glorious Word that gives us the strength (though not by magic) to do anything and everything incredibly well? Are we, the Church, truly exampling what it means to live in Christ? What of the Holy Spirit that lives in each of us who are called by Christ's Name? Are we exampling service an excellence not found anywhere else, but within the church walls? Does that sort of thing actually exist?

Hey worship pastors, leading worship is not so much about leading the musical volunteers on a Sunday morning, as much as it is assigning duties to them so they, in turn, become musical leaders themselves! Get to work!

When was the last time you heard of a worship pastor who

teaches his team music theory and song construction, but also insists that his/her team members take ongoing, private (professional) music lessons in order to become more proficient musicians and singers? Have you ever heard of a music pastor appointing the most well rounded members of their teams to begin discipling (mentoring) the teams younger and less musically able members? What about actual auditions for a place on the worship team that entails the presentation of a song by the auditioning person followed by a brief Q&A between the music pastor/worship leader and the potential member, so both parties understand the roles and rules of this appointment? Aren't these questions very good questions to ask? Why aren't these questions being asked?

These are things that should absolutely happen in every church that has a worship team! Though, rarely does this type of accountability actually occur as a result of accepting an invitation to participate. That's really too bad. But, this may be another small issue that speaks to why the church is such a failure at the musical (and overall) mission we've been given.

How did we go from creating the University, building the musical alphabet and canonizing the first written music; creating and teaching a viable music theory, and enlisting the greatest composers known to humankind to present quality music to a worshiping congregation… to how the average church functions musically today?

Along with that, why is it completely acceptable to enjoy "Jesu – Joy of Man's Desiring", and not Sting's "Fragile" during offertory? Actually, I've presented an instrumental, and very well arranged, version of that particular popular tune during offertory and witnessed a congregation in deep worship during the presentation! It's a beautiful tune, and maybe the Lord also enjoys that tune. I am making a commentary about how music can be a wonderful tool... if used correctly and by able musicians.

The pastor of the large, affluent congregation that enjoyed "Fragile" didn't go on-and-on about the music being a "Sting tune" before we presented it. Because that simply wasn't the point! Take note that many of the parishioners were fully aware of the tune we were playing... and those who were hip to the matter worshiped because of the beautiful arrangement and the message of the tune itself! There were several great compliments to the players and the arranger after the service,

"Wow! I would not have expected that! I'll never hear that song the same way again!"

Perfect. The exercise accomplished far more than some spotty version of whatever tune played badly, or by church players who play poorly – whether, or not, the "more Christian" tune featured

Jesus' great Name in the title! Right? This particular incident was one of my favorite times in worship over the past 30+ years, and I've since participated in other presentations of well-known popular songs arranged for offering. It goes over really well, when it's arranged well and played well. That's music, and what musical presentation should be, in a nutshell.

Interesting to this story's point is the fact that the musicians who comprised the worship team at that church on that Sunday were from the pool of regularly gigging professional musicians living in the Denver metropolitan area, and that particular arrangement was written by a good friend who was also in the process of receiving his Doctorate from CU! I truly enjoyed playing at that church, and from week-to-week one could only guess what type of great music we would be presented with – as to be a member of the team, you had to be a proficient music reader and a skilled player. The church's worship pastor was (and is) a great writer, vocalist, keyboardist and arranger and he wrote parts that challenged us each week during my eighteen months playing at that church. More importantly, he let us play the way we were meant to play our instruments! We were there (in the church's employ) because of how we played and how we worshiped through our playing! Actual musicians! Imagine that! As a result, we were able to take that congregation to wonderful heights in worship. Not so much because each of us considered ourselves "great people" or a "great team". But, because we understood that each of us was meant to do the job we performed there! We also understood that it is easy to worship and present worship in an environment where everyone knows his or her individual and musical job! Understanding always makes a truer and more agile and adept worship team! Always! As a result of having those basic concepts together as a church, I dare say that congregation was treated to greater heights in worship than our musically struggling neighboring fellowships! The pastor of the church was often asked "how…?" by his neighboring pastors, and he very forthrightly spoke about the musical vision he was given at the church's foundation, and his means of accomplishing the daunting task of achieving it. He often chatted with us about how shocked and often offended his neighboring pastors were in their response to his very simple approach of hiring great musicians!

Then again, this particular pastor is revolutionary in many ways. This particular church has been, to date, the only place I've heard a pastor tell the congregation to give only five percent tithe, and give the other five percent to a family helps ministry! This large (thousands) church with a full staff, counselors, paid musicians and new buildings going up all over the Denver Metropolitan area wasn't demanding more funds! This church was also employing musicians to be musicians! The blessing of the Lord I saw there put titanium in my spine to challenge all churches to seek the

Lord's vision and then to live by that vision whether or not earthly success becomes their story. To date, I can only site three instances (each operating in my personal history for less than three years each) where I felt honored to belong to a church, while playing with players I loved playing with! Other than those specific times in my life, my time on worship teams has been a lot of unnecessary work just to make the songs presentable. These small periods of time, these "islands of blessing", have kept me working in the church, and when they occur it reminds me of what musical worship is supposed to be for those of us called to present musical worship in the church!

"Fragile" (Nothing Like The Sun 1987 A&M Records Inc.) – written and arranged by Sting. All songs published by Magnetic Publishing Ltd. Represented by Regatta Music/Illegal songs, Inc. (BMI)

Chapter 9

I have mentioned that I have worked for many years in the "secular" music community (often amongst fellow Christians who have also chosen to work there instead of within the church). Along the way, I've come to understand that there are strong reasons why some of the world's more able Christian musicians aren't showing-up to participate in the worship program of their local church. As I've walked and talked with many of these displaced lilies, I've learned that there is an apparent misunderstanding and complete disconnect between the musician and the "musical worship sub-culture" that the church has become.

The lack of able musicians and artists in the average fellowship may have to do with a church's almost ugly and distasteful perception of the music and arts culture.

In my own experience, the church can be downright hostile toward musicians! Yes, musicians are weird, and they don't think like the average sheep (whomever they are). I think the average church staff looks upon the musician as somehow "rebellious" or "unwilling to fit in". As a musician, I ask the question, "fit into what?"

The musician's often-cynical perception of the average church service looks a lot like this:

- 20-to-30 minutes of often very poorly played music

- An earnest request for money (often pertaining to some hackneyed and immature team-building quest), followed by announcements…

- To be finally summed-up by a person who is (at best) pretending to be 'friendly'; who then begins a discussion about some personal experience that may, or may not, culminate in how the matter is being handled through the speaker's faith, or through Biblical truth.

It is all very funny when looked at through the artistic mind, isn't it?

Then there are the musical participants in this presentation… The average worship team member is more likely to be onstage because he or she simply "enjoys participating", and/or they may "really like singing". Or, they have the thought of *"helping Jesus"*, or their interest begins and ends with somehow serving their local fellowship. All of these things are innocent enough as singular facets of personality. But, isn't it interesting that these people seek such a visible 'ministry', more so 'position', in their local fellowship(s)? Burying oneself in the "Toddler-through-5-Year" actual ministry is much less glamorous, isn't it?

The entire idea of able musicality and musical practice is most often lost on the average church player, while those of us who have spent years and even decades refining an actual musical or artistic gift through exacting intent are left outside of the music the church so mindlessly hopes to present. More often than not, there isn't a place for the true musician or artist within the worship program of the average church. Beyond this point, there are myriad unnecessary (and often hurtful) church policies that attempt to "rein in" the artistic mindset a true musician will undoubtedly possess. Is it alarming to anyone that those policies are usually written by persons who know nothing about music?

When faced with these very strange church policies, I've asked my accuser if they believe its 'okay' for a person who lacks Biblical knowledge, but who "really loooves to preach", to speak to the congregation on a Sunday morning? The response is, typically, a resounding "NO!" No? Really? I mean, a pedophile "loooves children" (albeit in a dark, twisted way), don't they? But, the understanding that they should never be released upon children is very clear. This issue of who should present music in the church is something of a muddied, stagnant puddle. Yet, it appears to be perfectly okay (if not expected, or normal) for a group of persons who cannot speak the Language of music, or who do not understand what it is to bring their real and actual offering to God in a sacrificial way, to lead the congregation in the act of musical worship? And they wonder why this isn't working?! HMMM…

Please understand, though I have had incredibly weird conversations with often-hostile pastoral staffers and congregants on this topic (more often than not!), I'm not slighting how the average church functions beyond the incredibly poor treatment of the average church's arts/music program. If it isn't plain to you yet… I care about very little else that constitutes the workings of a church. Nor, do I think something within the accounting department has much to do with why the music hurts my ears and my feelings. That is, unless there is some deeper, darker politics involved. But, I'm not talking about that! At least, not in this book…

Much of the church's confusion about music stems from an utter lack of Biblical foundation concerning *who is supposed to do what in the church* beyond the matters of Biblical teaching, preaching, and leading the fellowship as elders, deacons, and ministers. By "ministers" I particularly include staff members, counselors, ushers and those with the gift of hospitality and the caretakers of the fellowship's meeting place, and child-care providers.

This misunderstanding of who is a minister may be because the concept of leadership speaks to all aspects of guiding a fellowship's direction and should be considered with the same standard to which we hold our pastoral staff and elders. Imagine a church where everyone understands and performs their God-given assignments! Imagine a group of Christians who have sought Almighty God in the Name of Jesus to be equipped for the assignment the Lord has for each individual on earth under His Lordship – within and without the church?

More importantly, what if our personal calling has nothing to do with being visible within or without the church? How do you identify a lover of people? How do you identify kindheartedness and actual meekness? When was the last time you heard a message on loving everyone you come into contact with this week

– whether they get it, or not? I don't hear a lot about those "what we should be", or "how we should expect no reward for being who we should be" messages these days! Has the church really become so much about investment Christianity? It would appear so.

Luke 6:38 focuses on the word "give". Like many of you, I'm not able to give anything I do not possess. Also like many of you, most of what I have I've worked very hard to obtain. But, that IS the point, isn't it? If we do not posses something, it is impossible to give it to anyone!

As I mentioned before, I work hard to be the best musician I can be and it isn't always an easy task. Life happens to me, too. But, I know my job, and that provides a type of incentive as I work (sometimes wok hard) through an average day. Back to something I said earlier about my witness… the other thought that goes through my head when someone says, "I like your playing" has, at times, gone something like, "yeah… I spent hours this week trying to get my musical assignments together. It didn't go as well as I'd hoped it would!"

Through the years, I've learned to it isn't always about my accomplishments as much as it's about being in the practice chair to wrestle with music! That practice (there's that word again) keeps the blades sharp! But, what I'm discussing at this time is a human practice of music. Not an anointed gifting by the Lord. So… I guess that means we don't always bring victory to the platform every Sunday. Sometimes, we bring a struggle that resulted in a loss, of sorts. Many of us have experienced losses in our life struggle, as well as in our calling. But, that doesn't mean give up and stop fighting for what you asked for from the Lord the moment struggles arise! Keep fighting and be encouraged! Don't show up on the Sunday platform, if you haven't wrestled with music, in private and as a personal practice, from Tuesday through Saturday!

Now let's talk about whatever it is you are "good" at, and while we're at it let's include those things you are definitely not good at! Personally, I'm not very good with small children who aren't my own. Although I have truly enjoyed parenting my children through each stage of life, and I've learned a lot about babies and toddlers in the process… I would say that my bag of real-time accessible skills is left more than wanting when it comes to groups of other peoples' kids! My lack of enthusiasm has nothing to do with changing diapers, or being piddled upon by a small child! There are other, more drastic issues to contend with in life than that! So, the issue isn't 'fear'. Fortunately for me I've never felt a pang of guilt, nor have I felt the gentle prodding of the Holy Spirit, when a leader of the Children's Ministry stands before the congregation pleading with the progenitors of this sea of babies to participate in their care! As for dropping my own children off at the Toddler and Infant Ministry doors… I will say that Tracy and I always took our children to church with us, and kept each of them quiet in the sanctuary, throughout their infancy, while attending services. If the child became fussy, one of us took them out of the service, and returned when the child was changed, sleeping, fed, or otherwise satisfied. Plain and simple. That's parenting, and parenting isn't about someone else's discomfort because you have a child.

Back to being "good" at whatever… We should never operate out of any sort of fear in our lives. Whether that is a fear of mishandling a situation you're called to deal with, or the fear of being uninvited to participate in something you've never properly prepared for. At its core, life seems to be a simple matter of training for a task and allowing the Lord to place us in the environment that calls for the training we've been given. Right? I mean life is truly as simple as the situation David encountered with Goliath in 1 Samuel 17. Right? To some, David sounded really arrogant while he explained that both a lion and a bear had attempted to take sheep from his flock, and he had killed both animals for doing so. He then went forward to kill Goliath armed with the training he'd received while being a shepherd over his father Jesse's flocks.

Through my daily practice regimen, I have learned that music isn't magic, and that (for me) it is easy to understand and to apply the concepts of music while presenting it in any context. Because of my confidence through practice, I have been called arrogant. True. I am fallen. We are all fallen. But, the fact that I'm not afraid of music, or really care whether the listener likes me, music, or the music I have been given to present to the audience doesn't truly brand me as arrogant as much as it brands me as someone unlike the average church… anything.

Our calling as musicians has very little to do with the churches view of our skill set. However, this idea can only be understood through following the daily musical path that leads us to Sunday's presentation – as well as those other presentations of music throughout the week.

Not knowing how to properly hold a newborn is something a person would work on before jumping into the particular ministry of handling babies at the local fellowship. Right? Please understand that caring for those incapable of caring for themselves is, indeed, a ministry. That is why I cannot include the offering of music to a congregation in that particular category of definition. Offering music in the average church has simply become more about those offering, than the offering itself. In no way should a worship team ever feel that they received more from a worship service than those they've been called to lead in worship.

I've also found it more than a little convenient that the most difficult children in the nursery are the offspring of those visible and harried church staffers who are always happily handing their cranky, unfed, unchanged and largely undisciplined "lil' darlin's" to the volunteers of the Newborn and/or Toddler ministry… often while they run to the stage to give their weekly stirring rendition of some stinky song they can barely sing – because their week generally encompassed the care of the fellowship above their parental duty. Do you see the perfect irony?

The church has also erred greatly in understanding and living the differences between what is supposed to happen at home, and what is supposed to happen at church! In all cases, Christianity and Christian witness begins at home, above and beyond the position a person claims in the church. If you consider yourself a musician, your witness to your household begins with your personal spiritual and musical practice and a regular worship regimen amongst the regular duties of family and maintaining one's household.

Worship team members do not teach musical taste and/or maturity, musical integrity or musical accountability from the stage anymore than pastors display their lives from the pulpit. Have you ever wondered why so many "preacher's kids" go astray? Could it be because of the hypocrisy (not the failures) they see in the lives of their own parents? We must first example our faith and musicality at home and in front of those people living there. So, then, it is our lives that speak as witness above our often self-assigned duties. In the world of musicians, it isn't the presentation that proves you are a musician… it is only your focused practice at home, and in private, that witnesses truth to your claims of musicality.

When my children were much younger, my wife often missed seeing me perform. During that time I was often asked, "Where's your wife? Doesn't she like music?"

One Sunday morning a woman from our congregation asked Tracy why she "didn't bother coming?" to a gig I played with a notable Christian artist the week before. Of course, this individual was hoping to prompt some sort of spousal support. Or guilt – even though I hadn't asked her to defend or rescue me in any way! Busybody. My wonderful wife responded, "I listened to my husband rehearse the music for a week, at home. I didn't need to be there." Perfect. I love my wife.

The ill-defined concept of church ministry as it pertains to the musical aspect of church leadership has raged on for years, and in many different forms. But, other than the aspect of music, that is another topic for another book. Societally, we have come to many truths that allow the average, small church fellowship to function well – at least, on the surface.

Many churches wrestle with the idea that their poor musical presentation doesn't matter while simultaneously failing to attract the local un-churched population we have been called to reach out to. Instead of reaching the lost through the training of their people, a smaller fellowship may begrudge their community's larger fellowships that boast expensive lighting, sound, and props… As if these things are the point. Effectiveness has little (if anything) to do with how wealthy a church happens to be, financially. In both cases the music isn't very well presented, generally speaking. Presentation isn't about how the *show* (as in: "lights… action… camera…!") of church appears to an audience, as much as it is about the vision, credibility and abilities of those persons involved in the vision of the church, and how that is interpreted by the people groups the church hopes to reach out to. Maybe we really should be reaching out to the community at large through our lives… not through "how we appear", but simply from the standpoint of "who we are", and "how well we do it" within the community we live in. Once again, we have to escape the temptation to brand Christianity - while failing to be actual Christians beyond the branding of appearing Christian!

Maybe it really is more about how we handle ourselves when our ordered food isn't quite right – after we've shown who we are. After all, no one outside the church walls cares that we just performed to raging applause only moments before re-entering the real world.

Chapter 10

So… what do we do? This book isn't built simply to point out the obvious disparities between the church and the ever-growing mass of humanity who live outside its walls. However, it is obvious that the church needs a fresh coat of demolition and re-architecture in the area of musical worship.

The best first step might be gaining and executing an actual vision for the worship program in each, individual church that promotes its music as a means of reaching the lost community at large. If it is written, "without vision the people perish" (Proverbs 29:18)… the answer may very well lie partially in the making of a viable plan for our various music programs.

In an attempt to escape and evade the numerous and varied philosophies we could talk through concerning this matter, and the emotional mélange and mire such a conversation would unnecessarily bring into scope, let's instead begin to build a plan that can help us retake the earth Christ is returning to. Let's begin to build a plan to regain ourselves, and what it means to be called. Let's take a hard look at the work ahead and begin by taking the first steps toward uncompromising victory in Christ through the work the Lord called us to accomplish. After all, this is our home that God gave us. Right? This is our earth. Your part in "taking it back" is learning to do the job the Lord has given you to do! Star there! Novel idea, isn't it?

Okay. In order to devise a viable plan of action for the church's worship program, let's first (and foremost) consider the type of person who might be the best candidate for our worship teams. The first question might be something like, "what type of person would best fit here?"

Is the best candidate for the worship team a person who can play well, but who also has a basic articulation of their faith in Jesus Christ and his calling on their life? How profound should that person's articulation be as it compares to the mission statement of the church? Is there a mission statement about the worship program in your church?

The average church tends to first (and incorrectly) look at their resources in this and any other volunteer scenario, instead of seeking the Lord to fulfill the program's vision that is, hopefully, based upon prayer and the leading of the Holy Spirit as our Lord speaks to a particular fellowship through its leadership.

As evidence to previously made comments, I often find that there is no real vision to speak of, and the church begins most of their attempts to fill their worship teams by looking at the people who attend the church!

This tendency is what I'll refer to as "Mistake #1". If the church leaders refuse to lead its people, the most likely result is what is seen in churches across the country at this writing. So… why not build a plan, and ask (and expect) the Lord to fulfill the matter in the way only He can? Like most things in life, the Lord is waiting for us to ask what He can do with the virtual "nothingness" we face every day, and a hoped for vision of a viable worship program is no different than any other prayer!

The church enjoys programs that help us mend our finances, help us have better marriages, help us live healthier, and help us raise better children. But, there are very few (if any) programs that help churches build healthy and socially profound music/arts programs for the exact purpose of responding to the Lord's calling to the needs of actual and aspiring musicians who find themselves attending a given fellowship.

"Mistake #2", concerns the matter of the job description of worship leaders in the church. Why aren't worship leaders teaching their players to understand and present music at a high level?

The answer may have much to do with the lack of musical understanding by the worship leaders! Or, it's the lack of concerted effort by the church leadership to forge a viable music program! It always starts with the leadership, doesn't it? I mean, whether or not the particular effort to build a good musical environment is being hampered by the church's pastor is something more sinister, if not all too common.

The mistake I'm speaking to has to do with the false humility of the church leadership's mentality of "taking what their given", as far as the people who constitute the fellowship and therefore the teams that will function in the church. I can already hear the groans, "well, we don't have great players in our fellowship and we can't *make* our people take lessons, or ask them to be better musicians… Or, we won't have anybody who wants to participate in the worship program!"

Honestly, that may not be all bad! More to the point, have you ever considered that the lack of integrity and accountability on the part of church leadership is nothing more than a gross copout? Laziness strikes again!

Who says that people will rebel against the suggestion of actually meeting their church's vision? This isn't a matter of making anyone do anything they wouldn't naturally do… if they were led to do so! I would like to suggest that perhaps church leadership has acted like poor parents, who allow their children to run amok while in the futile hope that the child might "grow into" something wonderful. Without guidance (and the proper guidance at that!) the laziness and half-heartedness at the core of any volunteer church program will continue unless the discrepancy is spoken to. Which brings us to "Mistake #3"…

DON'T SETTLE for what's easily available in your fellowship, church leaders!! CHANGE IT! Joshua 1:3-7, folks! God is for us! Does it look bleak? Good! Watch what the Lord will do if we ask him to move the impossible! If your church has a single great musician, start there and build. One great player will draw other great players! By contrast, four lousy players won't draw anyone except other crappy players. I've tested this again and again and I've watched the Lord do incredible things with one player who knows their job.

The Lord has never told us to languish in any state of stunted growth! We are to be proactive and purposeful in our mission! Even if that means the worship has a single player who knows their job and does it. Stop throwing awful presentation at the platform while hoping for something great. It'll never happen. I know… I'm a musician. I would glad play with one musician who is an actual musician than with four weirdoes who think playing music on stage is about fellowship more than it is about music.

Mistake #3 is the incorrect idea that ignoring shoddy behavior is somehow "loving", and it is one of the grossest failures within the average church in America! Admittedly, the church can be a place where strange and domineering power plays are acted out. This is because the person at fault quickly learns that church is a place where standards are quelled by the overwhelming (and heinous) idea that there should be no standards for any hopeful participant!

For every musician I know who no longer attempts to play in their local church, there is a story about some opposing and too easily offended person who fears 'true' anything (particularly musicians) who attacked the pastor, elders, worship leader, and board members for their piece of the position pie in 'their' church in lieu of the more qualified musician.

Everyone wants to be seen as being important in the church body… even to the extent of stealing the seat of another person who should instead be in that place! The violation of Luke 14:8 is the order of the day throughout most of the church – especially in those smaller fellowships that dot our landscape. Meanwhile, leadership sits idly by and allows these noisy busybodies to govern the personalities and persons who will be seen as the church's functional "inner circle". It's disgraceful and it is very, very common.

These mistakes made by church leadership are legion, and it isn't hard to see how and why the church is failing as an outreach to our world. I'm only speaking to the area of music, and it's plain to see how other areas of common abasement could render a church wholly ineffective. So... CHANGE IT! Change takes a lot of hard work, and people don't like it. But, these changes may be necessary to achieve the vision we've been given by God Almighty.

Chapter 11

There Are Those Who Know...

There. I hope these concepts help you and your church grow in the area of musical practice and presentation. We've come to the end of the written portion of this book. Thanks again for hanging in there and looking deeply into the area of musical worship! I decided to end our time together by asking four of my friends and colleagues to weigh-in on the matter of musical worship. I've compiled the interviews in a roundtable style and I didn't edit the materials for content. I simply asked two professional Christian musicians and two worship leaders to speak to this issue in their own words. As I read their answers, I identified the prevailing thought that spiritual depth in addition to musical understanding should be a given equal consideration. This should shed a great deal of light on the subject and I hope you enjoy their commentary!

What is your personal definition of musical worship, and how does it function in your life?

Jonathan Moore – Pastor, Christian Life Church, Grenada, MS

Musical worship is a combination of God-centered music and/or lyrics that draws the individual and the corporate body into the near presence of God, to commune with Him. Whether singing, playing, listening, or in silence; I am able to make that journey and, if leading, help others make that journey with me.

Mark Vinciguerra – Luthier/Proprietor – Vinciguerra Custom Shop, Professional musician Palatka, FL

Worship is a vehicle to free your mind from the daily clutter and noise of our current circumstances, so we can get before throne of God to worship him… Freely!

Timothy Brinkman – Singer-Songwriter – Director/ Proprietor Fishers Artists Agency/ Director of music at New Life Church Davenport, IA

Musical worship is any kind of music aimed toward specifically blessing God. Much of the music I create and play serves this purpose. I write worship songs, lead worship at my church, and enjoy very much singing and playing worship.

Jeremiah Horner - Professional Musician, Producer/Proprietor
Audience of One, Worship Leader – Longmont, CO

I've always seen worship as involving sacrifice. We offer up our worship on the weekend but the sacrifice happens during the week.

How do you view your particular role in musical worship, and how does your "best result' affect the congregation you're leading in worship? Also, how does your role function in harmony with the congregation?

Jonathan Moore – Pastor, Christian Life Church, Grenada, MS

I see my role as a shepherd leading others to a place where I have already purposed to go – not driving people ahead of myself, but purposing to lead by example by being the lead worshipper. "The sheep know me and heed my voice" - Ideally a skilled worship leader is able to draw others to follow him or her into God's presence.

Mark Vinciguerra – Luthier/Proprietor – Vinciguerra Custom Shop,

Professional musician Palatka, FL

My role is to be a rock solid support to my fellow musicians, and give them a solid foundation under their musical feet. When you are playing in a situation that is "flowing", you do not have to think too hard. Thinking too hard is a distraction to the team and congregation, and it causes tension in the music that is ALWAYS felt by the congregation.

Timothy Brinkman – Singer-Songwriter – Director/ Proprietor Fishers Artists Agency/ Director of music at New Life Church Davenport, IA

My role is to create new songs that resonate with listeners and present themes about God in a truthful way, and to lead the congregation in a way that I don't become the target of attention. My role, at best, is for me to be simply singing with the congregation as we keep our focus on blessing God.

Jeremiah Horner - Professional Musician, Producer/Proprietor Audience of One, Worship Leader – Longmont, CO

I see my role in corporate musical worship basically the same as my role in any other musical situation: the music is happening, somewhere out there in the ether, and my job is to "plug-in" and contribute something. People can be inspired by quality, heartfelt music and inspiring people to worship is a big part of what I do.

The congregation contributes something back as well and when there is a room full of people in a spirit of worship, the fire can get big!

What type of musician would you like to see on the worship teams you lead?

Jonathan Moore – Pastor, Christian Life Church, Grenada, MS

Intuitive rather than purely professional – flexible and able to adjust and improvise.

Mark Vinciguerra – Luthier/Proprietor – Vinciguerra Custom Shop, Professional musician Palatka, FL

Excellent, but anointed!

Timothy Brinkman – Singer-Songwriter – Director/ Proprietor Fishers Artists Agency/ Director of music at New Life Church Davenport, IA

I love working with gifted musicians who can fluently play in many different styles and have a keen ear and an ability to create on the fly.

Jeremiah Horner - Professional Musician, Producer/Proprietor Audience of One, Worship Leader – Longmont, CO

Musicians who are growing both musically and spiritually. A person, regardless of skill level, can't have much to offer if they aren't learning and growing.

How effective is the amateur (volunteer) team versus the team of more able musicians in the area of musical worship?

Jonathan Moore – Pastor, Christian Life Church, Grenada, MS

I've never really worked extensively with 'professional' musicians in worship teams, but I have worked with sensitive players. An amateur team can be effective if worship is simple and organic – think Vineyard circa late '80's!

Mark Vinciguerra – Luthier/Proprietor – Vinciguerra Custom Shop, Professional musician Palatka, FL

Volunteer teams are tough because you always end up with one or two above average players (and vocalist), and a couple of weak players (and vocalist), with the rest being simply average at best. It is very hard for the above average players to play comfortably in this situation.

Timothy Brinkman – Singer-Songwriter – Director/ Proprietor Fishers Artists Agency/ Director of music at New Life Church Davenport, IA

While volunteer teams will seldom be able to compete with professional musicians in terms of raw musical ability, I've found that volunteer teams can be just as effective in leading worship as professional teams. The heart of worship is a sincere desire to bless God. Many of the most passionate and devoted teams I've seen and been a part of have been volunteer musician teams.

Jeremiah Horner - Professional Musician, Producer/Proprietor Audience of One, Worship Leader – Longmont, CO

I don't know that the two concepts have to be mutually exclusive. "Professional" is not necessarily "being paid," as a mindset. The team of musicians who are focused on contributing beyond themselves and equipped to do so is much more effective then the group of people attempting to gratify the self.

What type of persons would you like to see on the worship team you're currently leading?

Jonathan Moore – Pastor, Christian Life Church, Grenada, MS

I look for intuitive musicians, who can flow and adjust.

Mark Vinciguerra – Luthier/Proprietor – Vinciguerra Custom Shop, Professional musician Palatka, FL

Seasoned!

Timothy Brinkman – Singer-Songwriter – Director/ Proprietor Fishers Artists Agency/ Director of music at New Life Church Davenport, IA

I like working with sensitive, gentle, humble, caring people who love the Lord and love people.

Jeremiah Horner - Professional Musician, Producer/Proprietor Audience of One, Worship Leader – Longmont, CO

We should always be sharpening each other.

Do you feel it's important to lead the volunteers on your worship team toward private music lessons?

Jonathan Moore – Pastor, Christian Life Church, Grenada, MS

A certain proficiency is needed and all musicians should strive for excellence – but I would rather a worship team member was striving for spiritual excellence rather than technical mastery. Of course the more technically proficient a musician is the more creative the arrangements can be! But in corporate worship it seems to me it is more important that the congregation can participate rather than view as a spectator. I am concerned that people might come just to hear the worship band rather than enter in themselves. I strive for simplicity – pared down arrangements etc.

Mark Vinciguerra – Luthier/Proprietor – Vinciguerra Custom Shop, Professional musician Palatka, FL

Not as much as leading them to refine their playing skill by practicing and worshiping… A lot!

Timothy Brinkman – Singer-Songwriter – Director/ Proprietor Fishers Artists Agency/ Director of music at New Life Church Davenport, IA

I've never guided volunteers in this direction myself. But I currently lead a couple of my team members in private guitar lessons.

Jeremiah Horner - Professional Musician, Producer/Proprietor Audience of One, Worship Leader – Longmont, CO

I feel it's important for all of us as musicians to be constantly allowing ourselves to be pushed. Sometimes that involves lessons.

Given the opportunity, how would you present the idea of musical worship in the average Christian environment?

Jonathan Moore – Pastor, Christian Life Church, Grenada, MS

Without a lot of forethought and prayer, praise and worship is highly misunderstood. We have to present worship in such a way that people realign their understanding to Christ-centric worship (what He desires).

Mark Vinciguerra – Luthier/Proprietor – Vinciguerra Custom Shop, Professional musician Palatka, FL

Being from the deeper worship side of the average Christian environment, I have found that when worship is presented correctly, it will lead people to worship in a deeper place than they have ever been… regardless of the environment.

Timothy Brinkman – Singer-Songwriter – Director/ Proprietor Fishers Artists Agency/ Director of music at New Life Church Davenport, IA

I believe the best picture of musical worship is the notion that is, at its essence, a heaven-like experience. I don't believe that all we will do is worship God in heaven. But it is a big part of what we will do, and worshiping God together is one of the closest experiences we can have to that.

Jeremiah Horner - Professional Musician, Producer/Proprietor Audience of One, Worship Leader – Longmont, CO

Corporate musical worship is sort of a strange and unquantifiable phenomenon. I think as worship leaders we accomplish a couple of things: 1) the arts give us the ability to inspire people and to show them things they may not have otherwise seen.

2) The Bible says that if we are silent "the very stones will cry out!" As worship leaders, we help facilitate people coming together to "make a joyful noise."

Chapter 12

In the mid-1990's I created a business function as freelance contract worship music director, working with worship pastors to rebuild their in-house worship teams, and that assignment turned into a seven-year stint working for churches around the Denver metropolitan area. After the first year of halting contracts and hostile reactions from church players, I began to construct a "handbook" detailing the type of musical environment I desired to work in.

After building a viable template of the document I began sharing this handbook with forlorn worship pastors who then began to strongly suggest its reading to the participants on their teams. During this time, I also began presenting worship clinics around the country, and my "little booklet" started to make its rounds to various other churches through the clinics and seminars. Over time, this "worship handbook" became my working resume and several churches began to ask if they could purchase the template for their worship programs! I continue to sell this handbook to this day – nearly 20-years after writing the first draft. It hasn't changed much…

So, when tasked with writing this book, I decided to rework part of the handbook and present it here as a tool that could help any church move their team(s) to a better working scenario. I pray this helps your worship team! Enjoy!

Worship Handbook – X Church

Written by Brent-Anthony Johnson

Published 2012

By Brent-Anthony Johnson

Noisy Tony Music & Publishing

Table of Contents

Introduction

Who We Are

Pre-Qualifications

Service

Qualities of Leadership

Calling

Humility

Are We There, Yet?

Expectations (Core)

Expectations (Supporting)

Survey

Introduction

The purpose of this handbook is to provide an overview of the worship team function at X Church. In order to maintain the high level of musical ability and aptitude at X Church we strive to invite and engage musicians and vocalists who are called and who are musically and spiritually prepared for the task of leading musical and visual worship. This is not the volunteer-based worship team that is common in the average Evangelical church. Instead, we are striving to ensure that those entering our fellowship with an undeniable musical gift have an opportunity to worship and function with others who are equally called by God.

The Bible has a great deal to say about music and musical worship. Music is mentioned in at least 44 of its 66 books, and musical terms such as music, singing, and musical instruments (many specifically identified) are mentioned hundreds of times. One entire book, the Psalms, is given over to music and musical worship. In its original form, Psalms was a book of songs. We do not know how many passages in the prophetic books were originally sung. But many prophecies are written in poetic style, and it is thought that some prophecies were actually sung.

Who We Are

At X Church, we recognize that presenting musical worship is not "ministry" as much as it is a function of church leadership. Therefore, we believe in the development of those participating as a part of the worship team toward leadership of the congregation, with an eye to the church around the world. X Church desires to worship God as He desires to be worshiped. As we look to His word, we find many examples of worship that are becoming common to our corporate church experience, and we yearn to experience worship at the deepest level the Lord will make available to us as we continue to seek His will for our direction.

Pre-Qualifications:

- Be a worshiper and be able to verbally articulate the concept

  (John 4:23-24)

- Evident ability to play your instrument skillfully and a willingness to be auditioned by the team leader or assigned personnel.

- Demonstrate a willingness to hold this position with an "open hand".

- Be a faithful participant in the life of this church body as evidenced by regular attendance at small group gatherings and Sunday services.

- Demonstrate commitment to this body by becoming involved in growing, healthy relationships with other people who are growing here.

- Invest time and energy as evidence of your call to this body.

- Show a willingness to work within the expectations of the team leader.

- Indicate your willingness to support the team's vision beyond your personal or musical goals.

- Support of your spouse (if married) for involvement on the music team as either a musician or a vocalist.

- Willingness to pursue further education in music including Instrument, voice or music theory, if suggested by the team leader.

- Answer the Prospective Worship Team Member's Questionnaire included in this handbook.

Service

"People will never care how much we know, until they know how much we care..."

A musician and/or vocalist may be invited into service after he or she has met all of the requirements listed in the worship ministry handbook.

In calling for the listed pre-qualifications and commitments for participation in the worship ministry of X Church, it is our intention that there be a personal calling, an anointing, and a Godly desire evident in the participant. It is not our desire to make it difficult for "difficulty's sake", but rather to ensure and encourage proper attitudes, teachable spirit, Godly character, and the full array of God's gifts and calling in each team member - to the best of our ability. X Church has been blessed with a high level of musical ability, and we are committed to honoring and maintaining that blessing. We cannot over-emphasize the importance of regular personal musical practice for those who hope to truly "play skillfully".

In becoming a servant to earth's fallen humanity, Christ understood three very important matters that we in service should also understand:

Jesus knew *whom* He was and what He came to do on earth. Secondly, He understood that all things were given to Him and that His authority was absolute. Jesus also knew where His final destiny would lead Him (John 13:3). In other words, Jesus completely understands His true identity, true dignity, and true significance. He knows who He is, why He came here, and where He was going after He left here. Even more compelling, Jesus' own examples teach us His value system and how He worshiped more deeply in private than in public.

Each of us yearns to have significance and to make a difference in the part of the world we've been given to affect. However, in doing so, we must understand where we're supposed to serve, and what (if any) skills we should acquire in preparation for our service. It is very common for those with a lack of direction to seek the most dramatic and visible places to serve in the church body.

But, true service is simply an extension of the lives we're already leading; through those things that are already important to us… and those things we're already very well equipped to do. It is a matter of being, not becoming. It is through the lives we've been given that those most significant opportunities appear. Our job is far more about dying to ourselves than being seen by people. *"Whoever wants to be my disciple must deny themselves and take up their cross daily and follow me."* Luke 9:23

Qualities of Leadership

Proverbs 3:5-6 – *"Trust in the Lord with all your heart, and don't lean on your own understanding. In all your ways acknowledge him, and he will make your paths straight."*

Leadership qualities begin with a functional knowledge of God's Word and the regular pursuit of those traits found in His Word that define the character, attributes, and actions of God's people. For instance, a careful examination of a leader's qualifications reveal a person who has his or her private and public life in balance. Godly men and women understand that effective leadership flows from being deeply committed to prayer, self-assessment, and a sober understanding of what it means to lead under Almighty God. (Titus 1:6-8)

Once this is established in our lives, we begin to have an undeniable outward flow of who we have been created to be. *"(He) must be hospitable, one who loves what is good, who is self-controlled, upright, holy and disciplined."* Titus 1:9

"(An) overseer must be above reproach" (1 Timothy 3:2) and an *"elder must be blameless"* (Titus 1:6). While the traits identified by Paul in Titus and Timothy speak specifically to leaders of the church, any leader who possesses these traits would posses "God approved" leadership qualities.

Calling

As followers of Christ, the single most important commitment of our lives is, obviously, to the Lord. By engaging in the regular practice of pursuing the Lord, we begin to identify and define certain characteristics that are inherent to us as we seek to expand the Kingdom of God in the world we live in. These characteristics are the fingerprint of God on our lives, as He begins to show each of us how he intends to use us to reach the lost, and how we are to serve within His body!

In the same way, the definition of a potential leader in musical worship is a person whose life clearly speaks to the gifts they posses by God, and whose life practices speak loudly to the traits inherent in musicians and vocalists. In other words, a musician acts like a musician in the same way a person given to encouragement is known to be encouraging to those who know them.

The Old Testament defines a person's exceptional ability (skill) in a craft or art by the Hebrew word *Hokma*. In Exodus 31:3-5, God filled a man named Bezalel with the Holy Spirit and with *"skill, ability and knowledge in all kinds of crafts – to make artistic designs for work in gold, silver and bronze, to cut and set stones, to work in wood, and to engage in all kinds of craftsmanship."*

We all should be in the daily pursuit of the *hokma* the Lord has for each of us!

Humility

Do you know that to constantly say you're humble, or to constantly describe yourself as modest could actually be the evidence of a perverted form of pride?! The key to humility is to get our eyes off of ourselves and onto the One from whom, for whom and through who all things are!
(1 Cor 8:6 and Col1:16-20)

We must begin to understand that each of us is built with a specific purpose in the mind of God for His message to the fallen earth. If we do not come to understand what He wants to do in our lives, and that *that purpose is for others and not ourselves*, then we cannot expect to develop the discipline necessary to begin a personal journey with our Lord for His plan. What if each of us are responsible to seek the Lord for our earthly tasks – and volunteering for a position that we feel might bring us recognition is counter to His plan for us?

Are We There, Yet?

Musicians and vocalists who have expressed an interest in joining the worship team, and after meeting the team leader offsite, may be invited to attend (as a non-participant) weekly worship practices to observe the core worship team. This typically involves observing the core worship Team's pre-service procedure to corporate worship. The objective of the exercise for the non-participant is to learn the team's process and time-management skills.

The "support participant" phase may last from a few weeks to months, depending on the individual and the team's situation and/or need. This phase is used to reveal the individual's heart, desire, motivations, and calling – as communication is developed between the person and the team leader. There is no implication or promise that a supporting participant is a "regular part of the team", and this is simply another step in the process. As the process continues, the individual may be invited to play or sing along during practice – as an opportunity to see how the person blends with the current team, and to find their place in the musical environment.

This period may include a formal audition, which would include playing and/or singing two or more songs with minimal accompaniment. The audition may also be recorded for further review. At any point during this process either the individual or the team leader may decide that this is not the time to pursue regular involvement with the worship team. The hope is that by keeping this part of the process informal, any disappointment or embarrassment will be minimized should the situation simply not work out. But if everything goes well, this process may lead to participation at the supporting or core level.

Expectations - Core Musician/Vocalists:

- Working knowledge of God's Word.

- Teachable and pleasant disposition – with a willingness to serve the worship team.

- Reliable, on time, in-tune, warmed-up, and spiritually and musically prepared to perform the set.

- Regular personal music practice that promotes musical growth.

- Ability to follow a musical arrangement chart.

- Willingness to disciple Supporting musicians and/or vocalists if requested.

- Must be involved in a non-musical service at X Church (i.e. youth, nursery, hospitality, etc.)

- Thorough understanding of basic music theory and musical chart reading skills.

- Functional rhythmic and ear-training skills. (Possessing an absolute skill-set)

- Playing (tasteful musical interplay) with other musicians.

- Trained ear and able to play/sing proper notes, scales, chords, etc. as appropriate.

- Memorization of worship song forms.

- Ability to play a variety of styles of music.

- Ability to play "by ear" and develop a part in a short period of time.

- Maintain an organized songbook (chord sheet and/or

arrangement chart) and MP3s.

Expectations - Support Musician/Vocalists:

- Working knowledge of God's Word.

- Teachable and pleasant disposition – with a willingness to serve the worship team.

- Reliable, on time, in tune, warmed-up, and spiritually and musically prepared to perform the set.

- Ability to follow a musical arrangement chart.

- Must be involved in a non-musical service at X Church(i.e. youth, nursery, hospitality, etc.)

- Must be enrolled in weekly music/voice lessons with a trained professional instructor.

- Understanding rhythm, melodic taste and basic musical concepts.

- Maintain an organized songbook (chord sheet and/or arrangement chart) and MP3s.

Thank you for your interest in the worship program at X Church. We look forward to your continued involvement with our body as we worship the Lord corporately and through the many opportunities offered here! We have been blessed with a high level of musicianship and we are committed to honoring what the Lord is doing in this body.

Contact:

Name and contact information of Worship Director

Worship Participant Survey

Voice/Choir - Soprano ___ Alto ___ Tenor ___ Bass___

Music - Instrumental performance

Instruments? _____

Musical composition or arranging experience? _____

Visual arts - Prepare audio/visual presentations___ Photography ___ Painting ___ Sculpture ___ Banners____ Operation of Sound/AV equipment during worship services or other _____

Name _____

Address _____

_____

Phone (home) _____

Phone (cell) _____

Email address _____

Comments:

About The Author

Brent-Anthony Johnson is a professional musician, author, and life-long music student. He is also a husband, father, dog owner and homeowner. He loves and serves Jesus Christ - The Lord of heaven and earth. He and his family live in Northwestern Illinois.

Made in the USA
San Bernardino, CA
28 July 2014